Twayne's English Authors Series

Sylvia E. Bowman, *Editor*

INDIANA UNIVERSITY

Christopher Marlowe

Christopher Marlowe

by

ROBERT E. KNOLL
The University of Nebraska

Twayne Publishers, Inc.   ::   New York

For Virginia
Elizabeth
Sarah
Benjamin

CHRISTOPHER MARLOWE

Preface

THIS BOOK is a general, critical introduction to the works of Christopher Marlowe. Like the other volumes in Twayne's English Authors Series, it is addressed to the general reader, to beginning and more advanced students, and to teachers who are not specialists in Elizabethan studies. Each of Marlowe's works is considered in turn to show its interrelation of theme and structure. In each chapter requirements of form are given primary consideration; but, since form and idea are inseparably linked, one is not sacrificed to the other. In the chapters on the plays, stage action is emphasized; these plays are considered in their narrative sequence in order to show how the placing of scenes, speeches, and spectacles influence staged significance. Matters of rhetoric are discussed as they are part of the dramatic moment; and the poetry, aside from *Hero and Leander*, is not considered independently. The themes of the individual works are defined in contemporary terms; for this is a study in art, not in the history of ideas, politics, or poetics. Historical, political, theatrical, and intellectual matters are introduced only as necessary to explain individual passages and works.

It might be useful, at the outset, to indicate the general outline of this book. After an introductory chapter in which biographical facts and critical methods are set forth—Marlowe's life continues to attract general curiosity—the book considers Marlowe's translations, his earliest surviving work. These poems exhibit, however, the interests which engaged him throughout his whole writing career. His first poem, a version of Ovid's *Amores*, deals with sensuous worldliness; his second, a version of Lucan's *Civil Wars*, deals with violence, with power. These ideas are prominent in his first play, *Dido, Queen of Carthage*, where they are joined with praise of human nobility and dispraise of godly pettiness. In *Tamburlaine*, which is next considered, Marlowe dramatizes the recurrent human temptation to war; *Tamburlaine* turns out to be an apologia for the diabolical.

Doctor Faustus is again concerned with power; its protagonist illustrates the dangers, and nobility, of power unlimited by religion. *The Jew of Malta* opens questions of politics which are related to problems of power, but *The Jew* remains a scenario for the theater before it is a dramatic investigation of ideas. Like *The Jew, The Massacre at Paris,* the next play considered, raises questions of Machiavellianism as Marlowe chose to define it; but it is, unfortunately, the bare outline of a play, so abbreviated a text has come down to us. In *Edward II*, his last play, Marlowe turns his back on cosmological questions of purpose to center his attention on kings and rebels in a godless, political world. *Hero and Leander,* Marlowe's unfinished narrative poem, contains a number of his characteristic ideas and attitudes. A witty poem, it disparages the dignity of the gods and asserts the independence of human action. Like the plays, it is a work of great craft.

All Marlowe's work is singularly relevant to the twentieth century; for Marlowe, like us, is fascinated by power. Like us, he asks how authority can be restrained. He saw the ancient moral and religious limitations giving way, and he asks what in the nature of things limits the public ambitions of a Tamburlaine or the private ardors of a Leander. At the beginning of modern times, Marlowe asked the modern questions. He gave no settled answer.

ROBERT E. KNOLL

The University of Nebraska

Contents

CHRISTOPHER MARLOWE

by

ROBERT E. KNOLL

Christopher Marlowe's work is singularly relevant to the twentieth century; power fascinated him as it fascinates us. Observing that the ancient moral and religious laws were weakening, he saw that naked force was unchallenged in his day except by greater force. What in the nature of things, he asked, limits the ambitions of a Tamburlaine, the aspirations of a Faustus, and the ardors of a Leander? He asked, How can powder be restrained? and what authority sanctions restraints? At the beginning of modern times, he asked the modern questions. If he could give no settled answer, no one else has been able to do better.

This book is a general critical introduction to Marlowe's work, addressed to the beginning and more advanced students, and to the general reader. In it each of Marlowe's works is considered to show its interrelationship of structure and theme. The plays are carefully considered as orchestrations for the working theater, for Marlowe was one of the chief dramaturgical geniuses in English as well as one of its chief lyric poets. Since this is a study of Marlowe's art, not his mind or thought, matters of rhetoric, poetics, history, and biography are introduced only as necessary to clarify the ideas in the works before us. No polemic, this volume attempts to include the relevant Marlovian criticism and scholarship; and its footnotes and bibliographies will guide interested readers to contemporary controversies.

Chronology

ca. 1540	John Marlowe (Marley) born at Ospringe, near Faversham and Canterbury, son and grandson of tanners.
1560	John Marlowe in Canterbury, apprenticed to immigrant shoemaker named Garrard Rychardsson.
1561	On May 22 John Marlowe marries Catherine Arthur, daughter of William Arthur of Dover at St. George's Church.
1562	Mary, first of nine children, born to John and Catherine Marlowe; six of the nine survive infancy, four of them daughters.
1564	Christopher Marlowe born in Canterbury. Baptized at St. George's Church, February 26.
1573	Queen Elizabeth in Canterbury on state visit; holds court for two weeks. During year, several persons publicly executed within the city.
1579	January 14, Christopher Marlowe elected a Queen's Scholar at the King's School, Canterbury, which has a tradition of theatrical productions.
1580	December, Christopher Marlowe enters Corpus Christi College, Cambridge.
1581	March 17, matriculates. Succeeds to Archbishop Parker Scholarship in May, on the presumption that he intends to take holy orders.
1584	Receives Cambridge B. A.

ca.
1585   Translates Ovid's *Amores* and Lucan's *Wars.*
1584– Absences from College. Engages in secret government serv-
1586   ice (?).
ca.   *Dido, Queen of Carthage* written (with Nashe?). *Tambur-*
1586   *laine, Part One* written.
1587   March, leaves Cambridge. July, receives M.A. upon inter-
     vention of the Privy Council. October 2, 1587, letter from
     Utrecht to Lord Burghley mentions one "Morley" among gov-
     ernment messengers. Before November, *Tamburlaine Part
     One* acted by Lord Admiral's Company, possibly in inn-yard,
     with Edward Alleyn in title role. *Tamburlaine Part Two* fol-
     lows closely thereafter, possibly by November. *Historia von
     D. Iohañ Fausten* published in Frankfurt.
1588   Robert Greene in preface to *Perimedes the Blacksmith* refers
     to "that Atheist Tamburlan . . . blaspheming." *The Tragical
     History of Doctor Faustus* acted by the Lord Admiral's
     Men (?).
1589   February 28, "a ballad of the life and deathe of Doctor Faus-
     tus the great Cungerer" entered in Stationers' Register.
     August 23, Marlowe attacked by Greene in *Menaphon.* Sep-
     tember 18, Thomas Watson, coming to Marlowe's aid, kills
     William Bradley in a street fight. Both imprisoned at New-
     gate; Marlowe soon freed. Kyd's *Spanish Tragedy* acted (?).
     The Jew of Malta acted by Lord Admiral's Men.
1590   August 14, *Tamburlaine* entered in Stationers' Register and
     published "divided into two tragical discourses." Greene sneers
     at *Tamburlaine* in his *Farewell to Folly.*
1591   Early summer, Marlowe and Thomas Kyd share a study.
1592   *Edward II* acted by Pembroke's Men. Early in year Marlowe
     in government service at the siege of Rouen. June 23, Privy
     Council closes the London theaters on reports of rioting.
     Greene reproves Marlowe for "atheism" in *Groatsworth of
     Wit.* September 15, engaged in struggle with William Corkine,
     near the Chequers Inn, Canterbury. December 18, *Doctor
     Faustus* entered in Stationers' Register.
1593   January 26, *The Massacre at Paris* produced as "new" by Lord
     Strange's Men. May 12, Kyd arrested on charge of atheism;
     claims heretical tract in his possession belonged to Marlowe.
     May 18, warrant issued for Marlowe's arrest; apprehended at
     estate of Thomas Walsingham at Scadbury, Kent. May 20,
     answers charges to Privy Council; ordered to be in daily at-
     tendance on Council thereafter. May (or early June), Baines

gives Privy Council lengthy "Note" dealing with Marlowe's blasphemies. May 30, Marlowe killed in tavern brawl at Deptford by Ingram Frizer. June 1, coroner's jury of sixteen men acquits Frizer. June 28, pardon issued to Frizer on grounds of self-defense. July 6, *Edward II* entered in Stationers' Register. September 28, Marlowe's translation of Lucan's *First Book* and *Hero and Leander* entered in Stationers' Register.

1594   May 17, *The Jew of Malta* entered in Stationers' Register. *Edward II* and *Dido, Queen of Carthage* published.

ca.   Marlowe's translation of *Ovid's Elegies* published without date
1596   or license.

1597   Thomas Beard in *Theatre of God's Judgements* refers to Marlowe's death as illustrating "the admirable Judgments of God upon the transgressours of his commandements."

1598   Francis Meres repeats Beard's version of Marlowe's death. *Hero and Leander* published with dedication to Sir Thomas Walsingham by Edward Blount, the publisher; second edition later in year contains Chapman's continuation and Marlowe's poem divided into "sestiads."

1599   Marlowe's translation of *Ovid's Elegies* included in ecclesiastical censure and publicly burned.

1600   Marlowe's translation of *The First Book of Lucan* published in *England's Helicon* and in *England's Parnassus*. William Vaughan in *Golden Grove* provides new details concerning Marlowe's death.

1601   *The Massacre at Paris* published (?).

1602   Henslowe records paying four pounds to William Bird and Samuel Rowley "for their adicyones to doctor fostes."

1604   *The Tragical History of D. Faustus* published ("A-text").

1605   January 25, John Marlowe dies in Canterbury. May 17, Catherine Marlowe dies in Canterbury.

1608   *Doctor Faustus* forms part of English repertories in Germany.

1616   An enlarged and altered edition of *Doctor Faustus* published ("B-text")

1633   *The Famous Tragedy of the Rich Jew of Malta* revived at Cockpit and Court Theaters and then published.

CHAPTER 1

The Man and His Work

I *The Marlowe Problems*

CHRISTOPHER MARLOWE has caught the imagination of
the modern reader. Among his literary contemporaries only
Shakespeare is better known. His public name easily eclipses
Ben Jonson's, Edmund Spenser's, and John Donne's; and seekers
after notoriety who have exploited Shakespeare now seem bent
on exploiting him. It is relatively easy to see why. For one thing,
Marlowe's lyric "The Passionate Shepherd to his Love" is exceedingly famous; it expresses our yearning for lost innocence:

> Come live with me, and be my love,
> And we will all the pleasures prove
> That hills and valleys, dales and fields,
> And all the craggy mountains yields.
>
> And we will sit upon the rocks,
> Seeing the shepherds feed their flocks
> By shallow rivers, to whose falls
> Melodious birds sing madrigals. . . .

The poem is a standard piece of English verse. In addition to the
poem, Marlowe's play, *The Tragical History of the Life and
Death of Doctor Faustus,* is often anthologized and frequently
produced. Its protagonist, Doctor Faustus, has become part of

modern mythology. Goethe chose Faustus as the protagonist for his masterwork, and Oswald Spengler saw in him the spirit of Western culture. Spengler called this the "Faustian Age." "The new *Faustian* world feeling," he said, referring to the figure of Faust found in Marlowe, Goethe, and others, is "the new personal experience of *the Ego in the Infinite*."[1] Poets like Karl Shapiro and novelists like Saul Bellow, as well as editors of *Time* and the *New Yorker*, refer to the learned doctor casually, confident that their readers will understand their allusions. For the general reader, as for students and writers, Faustus' story dramatizes not only what modern scientific inquiry does *for* us but ultimately what it does, or can do, *to* us.[2] Like the celebrated lyric, *Doctor Faustus* deals with the loss of innocence.

Marlowe's modern ideas are not contained in a single play, however masterful. By the time he met his violent death at the age of twenty-nine, he had written seven plays and a major narrative poem, plus a number of lyrics which are now lost. All of his writing has a startling relevance to the twentieth century, for in play after play Marlowe defines the conflict between ambition and responsibility, between power and morality. He poses the central question: What but religion can restrain power? What but moral force can restrain physical force? The very survival of our civilization depends on the answer we find for the question that Marlowe insistently asked nearly four hundred years ago. His plays are unmatched in English in their imaginative comprehension of the modern dilemma.

As works of art, the plays and poems are more than documents in the history of ideas, for they have an esthetic life of their own. *Tamburlaine* invites a participation in a mode of being almost never successfully dramatized. When we read the play, we sink ourselves into the diabolical; for a time we experience the satanic in a kind of adolescent daydream of total power. In *Doctor Faustus* we enter a world of total knowledge, where all facts are at our command, where all secrets are ours for use. In this play we learn how it feels to come out at the back of the north wind, and we learn what questions await answering there. In *The Jew of Malta* we participate in Machiavellian politics, and in *Edward II* we are in a world of historical accident, where there are no gods. The plays are written in some of the most eloquent poetry in English drama; they are filled with recognizable human beings;

and they are skillfully plotted to provide suspense and excitement. Moreover, they contain a comprehension of experience which we quickly recognize as singularly Marlovian. Beyond each page we detect an imaginative presence, a poet with an original perception and expression.

This imaginative presence is subjective in an unElizabethan way. Coming to the poetry from Spenser and Sir Philip Sidney, or from Shakespeare and Jonson, we are surprised to find ourselves aware of the person of the poet, his mind, and his prejudices. Renaissance poets are usually more nearly anonymous. Unlike Shakespeare, Marlowe's dramatis personae seem intermittently but occasionally to be his spokesmen. We are not free to identify Marlowe with Tamburlaine or Doctor Faustus or any character in any play. But, when we read the plays, we feel that we know something of the playwright because of the nature of the questions which the plays insistently raise. The speeches often have an intensity beyond scenic requirements, a particular intensity that takes us back to the playwright; and the facts of Marlowe's short, spectacular career reinforce the sense of his character which the plays provide. His life and work are of a single piece; for, in and out of the theater, he was a bold man, unafraid of attacking the shibboleths of his time.

Marlowe's life contains unsolved mysteries which invite cloak and dagger speculations. The chief puzzle is his death. Was he in point of fact accidentally killed in a tavern brawl as his drinking companions maintained, or was he assassinated? If he were murdered, why? And by whom? Exactly what "underworld" connections had he? And what precise connections did he have with the powerful circles within Queen Elizabeth's court? What kind of man was this who had an imaginative comprehension of the dilemma of all times and yet involved himself in current political intrigue? If Marlowe's literary work reads like a prolegomenon to the modern world, his life story reads like an uncompleted thriller. In addition, it may help us understand his poems and plays.

II *The Life*

Christopher Marlowe was born February 26, 1564 in Canterbury, then as now a busy cathedral city. During the Reformation, the Cathedral fell from its greatest wealth; before 1540 its shrine of St. Thomas à Becket could be described by Erasmus in hyperbole: "the least valuable portion was gold; every part glistened, shone and sparkled with rare and very large jewels, some of them exceeding the size of a goose's egg."³ The riches of the city were enough in Marlowe's youth to inspire a sensitive imagination, and in 1573, when Queen Elizabeth herself came on a state· visit, she held court in Canterbury for a fortnight. Young Christopher must have heard her bells and trumpets, seen her sergeants-at-arms, footmen, marshals, and messengers; and he may even have seen her proceed into the Cathedral under a canopy "borne by four of her temporal knights." Her banquets at the archbishop's palace must have been the talk of the prosperous city. The city was also brutal. Hangings were public in Marlowe's day—the gallows stood outside St. George's Gate; and trials for witchcraft were not unknown.

Marlowe was born into a family of leatherworkers. Although this was "a rather prosperous guild in sixteenth century Canterbury"⁴ Marlowe's family was never very well off. His ancestors were a quarrelsome and litigious lot, and their antics fill a good number of pages in the local records; his immediate family was no less colorful. His sister Ann was said by her churchwardens in 1603 to be a "malicious uncharitable person seeking the unjust vexation of her neighbours." She was "a scold, common swearer and blasphemer of the name of God. . . ." In later years Christopher himself got a reputation for blasphemy. Dorothy, another sister, was also celebrated in Canterbury. Within a few months after her marriage to Thomas Graddell (1594), the husband complained that a man named Brown was boasting of favors conceded him by Dorothy. As a result of the legal proceedings that followed, Graddell was excommunicated and imprisoned for failure to pay court costs. "A multitudinous sea of disturbances ever followed the Graddells," the archivist of Canterbury has recently written.⁵ Christopher's father also disturbed local tranquillity. The court records indicate that he was noisy, self-assertive, and improvident, endlessly engaged in lawsuits, usually as a defendant for debt. He was able to take apprentices, but they too seem to have been troublesome. Three of them were involved in bastardy cases, one with Mrs. Marlowe's maid.

Catherine Marlowe had married John in 1561 when he was still
an apprentice; her death in 1605 followed his by only seven
weeks, and, in accordance with her request, she was laid to rest
"near where as my husband John Marlowe was buried." Her
modest bequests promptly started her family quarreling.

Christopher Marlowe entered the King's School, Canterbury,
at the New Year, 1579. It is rather strange that he was not
elected before this—he was nearly fifteen years old, the upper
age limit for entering students.[6] The school, which enjoyed a
brilliant reputation, was a center of theatrical interests. Its head-
master had a large private library including a number of volumes which have been claimed as sources for Marlowe's plays.
Young Marlowe early and uncritically read the medieval romances then popular,[7] romances that contained enough bloodshed and rapine for any adolescent, and invited the reader to
take delight in gore for its own sake. A generation earlier Roger
Ascham, the schoolmaster, had warned readers away from them,
and by Marlowe's day, they were a little outside the approved
canon of reading. After two years, in 1581, young Marlowe
moved to Corpus Christi College, Cambridge, where he remained for six years. A year or so older than many matriculants,
Marlowe was "a rare scholar" who "made excellent verses in
Latin."[9] For the next six years he was a "Canterbury scholar,"
for he had been given one of the three scholarships established
by the will of Archbishop Matthew Parker for candidates dis-
posed to enter holy orders. In 1584 he received his bachelor's
degree.

During his Cambridge years, Marlowe was absent from college for weeks and even months at a time. It is now generally
assumed that in some of these periods he was involved in yet
undisclosed government service either as a secret agent or as
a confidential messenger. His activities brought him into dis-
favor with the academic authorities and caused him to be suspected of Catholicism, a capital crime in those tense years before
the Spanish Armada. When he supplicated for the master's
degree in 1587, the university proposed to withhold it. The
academic authorities were forced to yield only when Queen
Elizabeth's Privy Council intervened.

We can learn something of Marlowe's governmental activities

from the letter of the Privy Council to Cambridge on his behalf. Though it had been reported that "Christopher Marley" was determined to go to Rheims—a center of Catholic activity—the Council wanted it understood that the young man had done Her Majesty good service: "It was not her Majesty's pleasure that anyone employed as he had been in matters touching the benefit of his country should be defamed by those that are ignorant in the affairs he went about."[10] Marlowe must have been employed by Sir Francis Walsingham, the Queen's powerful Secretary of State, who was in charge of an elaborate espionage system. In time Thomas Walsingham, his cousin, became Marlowe's patron and close friend—they had both been in the Secretary's employ. Marlowe may also have been used by Lord Burghley, the Queen's chief adviser and the chancellor of Cambridge University, in similar capacity on other occasions.[11] In any case, thanks to the intervention of powerful friends, Marlowe's master's degree was conferred in July, 1587.

Except for brief periods, Marlowe spent the rest of his short life in and around London. He brought his plays *Dido, Queen of Carthage* and *Tamburlaine* to town with him. His translations of Ovid and Lucan and the *Dido* were apprentice pieces; the *Tamburlaine* was not. Very likely *Tamburlaine Part One* was produced by November, 1587, and *Part Two* very shortly after *Part One*. The two plays made his reputation; and within a year Robert Greene, a Cambridge man now living by his pen and his wits, complained publicly that Marlowe was "daring God out of heaven with that Atheist *Tamburlaine*."[12] In the next year, and then again in 1592, Greene attacked him even more vigorously. It might be added that Greene in spite of his sneers imitated Marlowe to the best of his considerable ability.[13]

Marlowe's life in London was hardly a quiet one. By 1589 he was living in Norton Folgate, near the theaters, close to Thomas Watson, the poet. In September, Marlowe and one William Bradley fell to fighting in Hog Lane, whereupon Watson came to Marlowe's rescue. In the ensuing brawl Watson fatally stabbed Bradley. Though Marlowe fled the scene, both he and Watson were imprisoned in Newgate: Marlowe for two weeks; Watson for a somewhat longer time. In December, Marlowe presented himself at the Old Bailey and was discharged. Watson was finally discharged the following February on the grounds that he had killed Bradley in self-defense.[14]

By 1591 Marlowe had become one of a group of intellectuals and bohemians. Among them was Thomas Hariot, the most distinguished English mathematician of his time; William Warner, Hariot's disciple (another William Warner was a poet); Matthew Roydon, a poet whose great promise seems never to have been fulfilled; and Edward Blount, the bookseller who later formed one of the syndicate to publish Shakespeare's First Folio. Walter Raleigh and Thomas Walsingham were associated with this circle, if it were ever anything so formal as a "circle." In the early summer of 1591 Thomas Kyd and Marlowe shared a room which they used as a study for writing. Several years earlier—at about the time of Marlowe's appearance with *Tamburlaine,* but of this there is scholarly contention—Kyd had had an enormous success with his *Spanish Tragedy;* and both young men were under the patronage of Thomas Walsingham. Two years after sharing the study with Marlowe, on May 12, 1593, Kyd was arrested and questioned concerning his heterodox views on religion. These were described by the authorities as "vile heretical conceits denying the deity of Jesus Christ our Saviour."[15] On the rack, Kyd asserted that the paper upon which the judgment was based did not belong to him; it was Marlowe's. His and Marlowe's papers had become confused in their shared writing room. When questioned further, Kyd wrote to the Lord Keeper about Marlowe's "monstrous opinions": "First it was his custom when I knew him first—and as I hear say he continued it in table talk or otherwise—to jest at the divine scriptures, gibe at prayers, and strive in argument to frustrate and confute what had been spoke or writ by prophets and such holy men." Kyd also reported that Marlowe maintained that "our savior Christ" loved St. John with "an extraordinary love"; that St. Paul was "a Jugler"; and that "things esteemed to be done by divine power might have as well been done by observation of men."[16] Expression of such heterodox opinion was a capital offense in Elizabethan times.

On May 18, a warrant was issued by the Privy Council for Marlowe's arrest. On May 20 he appeared; but instead of prison and torture—what Kyd had received—he was "commanded to give his daily attendance on their Lordships until he shall be licensed to the contrary."[17] Apparently Marlowe's friends did not forsake him, and perhaps it is important that he was apprehended in the home of Thomas Walsingham at Scadbury. Walsingham was in favor with the Queen—she was later to visit and knight him at Scadbury.

But Marlowe was not yet out of trouble. A certain Richard Baines delivered a "Note" to the Privy Council later in May (presumably) concerning this "atheist" Marlowe. It contained a good number of startling charges based on hearsay: "Almost into every Company he cometh he persuades men to Atheism willing them not to be afeard of bugbears and hobgoblins," Baines wrote. "The first beginning of Religion was only to keep men in awe." Baines asserts, among other things, that Marlowe was skeptical of important details in the Old Testament, thought that the New Testament was "filthily written" (he probably meant that its Greek was not Classical), and held that "all protestants are hypocritical asses." We can perhaps catch the temper of Baines and, behind him, Marlowe in the report that Marlowe said that "all they that love not tobacco and boys were fools."[18] The rope on Marlowe appeared to be tightening; but before he could be called to answer these new accusations, he met his violent death.

On May 30, 1593, Marlowe went with friends and acquaintances of the Walsingham circle to Deptford, a village downstream from London. One of the company, Ingram Frizer, was a man of property and Lady Walsingham's business agent. Another, Robert Poley, had been frequently employed in secret missions for the government; and the third was Nicholas Skeres, a man of some substance and a friend of Marlowe's friend Roydon. The four men dined at Eleanor Bull's tavern, spent the afternoon quietly talking in her garden, and afterward went inside to supper. A dispute concerning the reckoning arose, and in a passion Marlowe drew Frizer's dagger and gave him a couple of cuts on the head. In the struggle that followed Marlowe received his death wound above his right eye. A coroner's inquest was held on June 1—the details of the activities of the day come from this report—and a jury of sixteen men quickly acquitted Frizer.[19] There is reason to believe, however, that the coroner's inquest was hurried, the report incomplete, and the whole matter hushed up. We are, of course, free to wonder why. And so Christopher Marlowe died, age twenty-nine. From the records of his life, we can perceive the general outline of his character. A genius, he was of that critical temper which insists on examining what the timid hesitate to acknowledge even exists; and so he tried to submit the sacrosanct to the test of common sense. Irritable and vexatious in person, he may or may not have been an atheist and a pederast; but he considered the possibility of such things—he had a streak of the exhibitionist in him. In a rather adolescent fashion he set out to shock all those who were shockable. No cruelty was too gross for him to consider, no inclination too unnatural for him to discuss. He lacked tenderness, and although the only love he knew was self-fulfillment, wherever he went, he was the center of the circle, the subject of the conversation, the object of fear. We can wonder if Marlowe's talent would have matured as Shakespeare's did; but, again, we can only speculate. We are sure that his early death was a major loss to English literature.

III   *The Scholarship*

Although Marlowe has been acknowledged for nearly two centuries, at least, as Shakespeare's chief early dramatic contemporary, there is no general agreement concerning the meaning of his plays and poems. The controversy rages in classrooms and in scholarly journals; and the issues are clear: Are these plays Christian or are they attacks on Christian orthodoxy? Does Marlowe invite us to embrace a Faustian world of aspiration or does he preach a medieval *contemptu mundi*? Some students think these plays dramatize current religious issues and give full measure to both iconoclastic temptations and conventional responses. Certainly Marlowe provides vivid representations of the world, the flesh, and the devil; but he also invites us to question Christian orthodoxy. Some critics hold, as I do, that Marlowe, being neither a melodramatist nor a preacher, provides a persuasive dramatic statement of what attracts us away from Christianity—even as he shows the dangers of departing from it. In this way he is the prototypical figure of the Renaissance in England.

When we set out to understand these plays and poems, we are confronted with difficulties, the chief of which is the text itself. Unhappily the text of only two of the plays—the two parts of *Tamburlaine*—were published during his lifetime; and the texts of all are badly produced or printed. They are so filled with obvious errors that some think they are mere wrecks of plays, the ruins of works now irretrievably lost. Recently other scholars have begun to think that, for all their imperfections, they are substantially what left Marlowe's hand and that their corruption is evidence of his youthful impatience or indecision. The problem is unresolved; but until new evidence appears, we have to accept the fullest texts as Marlowe's completest statements.

But the texts are not the only problems; we cannot be sure in what order these plays were composed, for the initial publications of most were long delayed and sixteenth-century references are confused. We can be reasonably confident that *Tamburlaine* was first acted in London, but we do not know where or exactly when; and nobody can be sure whether *Faustus* is an early or a late play. We can, therefore, only with common sense hypothesize an order of composition from what internal and external evidence we possess.

Having accepted a text and a chronology, if we are to understand the dramatic significance of each play, we must analyze its dramaturgy. We need to determine at each point in the action of each play where Marlowe intends our sympathies to lie; and we must consider the movement of our sympathies throughout the total action. Only then can we capture the general drift of dramatic meaning. If Marlowe the dramatist cannot guide our sympathies—that is, control our responses to his drama—the plays are pieces of antiquarian interest only. Eugene Waith has recently written: "Although Marlowe's devices for qualifying or shifting opinion, for distancing characters or encouraging us to take them to our bosoms, are not uniformly successful, their virtuosity can always be admired, and they can be seen to great advantage even in a play in which they do not work perfectly."[20]

In addition to the careful scrutiny of the text, we can get

some help in understanding the plays from another source. Given a puzzle which no worrying of lines can solve, we can look at the other works from Marlowe's hand, for often the plays can illuminate one another. If even then a passage or a play remains obscure, we may turn to Marlowe's life and times. Sometimes even gossip can guide us to the resolution of obscurity. As Harry Levin says, "We should pay little attention to such hearsay if it did not underline tendencies which, we shall notice, are writ large throughout his work."[21]

Marlowe has inspired a good deal of scholarship. His plays have been more frequently edited than those of any Elizabethan except Shakespeare, and he has attracted biographers both popular and scholarly in good number. Within the last two decades a number of monographs dealing with his relationship to his dramatic and intellectual predecessors have shown us his place in Elizabethan theatrical and intellectual history; and critics have explicated individual plays, often with helpful results.[22] The object of this study differs in degree rather than in kind from what has been done before. Since Marlowe has not always been recognized for his dramaturgical maturity, we will examine the dramatic organization of the plays in what we may assume to be their chronological order. Necessarily we will be involved in defining their themes, for they inform the organization; but we will be more concerned with the plays as works of art, as orchestrations for the theater, than as documents in the history of ideas. We will observe how Marlowe's stage techniques and ideas changed during his short career. This book will have fulfilled its purpose if as a result of its analysis of the poems and plays it sends its readers back to the works themselves.

CHAPTER 2

Apprenticeship: Ovid, Lucan and Dido, Queen of Carthage

I *The Translations*

MARLOWE'S FIRST POEMS were translations of Ovid and Lucan; and, although neither can now engage our attention in its own right, both indicate the direction of Marlowe's early interest. The translation of Ovid's *Amores,* generally assumed to be Marlowe's earliest surviving work, was probably made before March, 1587, when he left Cambridge permanently. Ovid was to remain his favorite poet throughout his short life, as he was the favorite Roman poet of the young men about town in those days. The *Amores*—Marlowe called them "elegies" because they are written in the Latin elegiac verse— are a series of forty-eight satiric and frivolous meditations on erotic love. In them, "Ovid is bent on representing every phase and situation of love, every twist and paradox of love's psychology"; and Marlowe surrenders himself to their impudence with gusto.[1] His translations, the *Elegies,* had a considerable vogue: Nashe quotes from them in *Jack Wilton* (1594), Thomas Bastard alludes to them in *Christoleros* (1598), and Ben Jonson lifts and characteristically "corrects" one for inclusion in his *Poetaster* (1601). Some scholars even see an echo of Marlowe's *Elegies* in Shakespeare's *Merchant of Venice* (1596?).[2]

The *Elegies* went through at least six early editions, all surreptitious, but we may assume that Marlowe himself had no part in their publication and that he regarded them as the juvenilia they are. Though all are undated and claim Middleburgh, Holland, as their place of publication, the earliest were probably printed in London by W. Jaggard. In 1599 Jaggard brought out the pirated anthology of poems entitled *The Passionate Pilgrim* attributed to Shakespeare, but he also published the Shakespeare First Folio in 1623. Two of the early editions of the *Elegies* contain only ten of the more licentious of the elegies; two other editions give complete texts of the translations and apparently were printed in the last years of the 1590's. Copies of Marlowe's Ovidian elegies were burned publicly on June 4, 1599, by order of the archbishop of Canterbury and of the bishop of London in their attempt to correct the satirical temper of the time. Yet two more editions of the translation appeared late in the seventeenth century. All of the editions are filled with blunders that result from hasty printing. This first work may be regarded as rather characteristic of Marlowe. Defiant of authority, it is licentious, youthful, and vigorous. These *Elegies* were an anathema to the Elizabethan establishment, but they delighted the young men.

The *Elegies* give us opportunity to examine other attitudes of the very youthful Marlowe. First, despite the popularity of the *Amores*, we are struck by this choice of subject because Marlowe was supported at Cambridge by one of Archbishop Parker's scholarships for those who expected to enter the clergy; on the evidence of the *Elegies*, we must assume that Marlowe was a most unascetic student of theology. Although we know that even theologians have their saturnalian moments, we are perhaps taken aback not simply by the frankly erotic nature of Marlowe's Ovid but by the translator's unapologetic delight in eroticism. This apprentice clergyman was not only sensuous, he was worldly. For centuries Ovid's poetry had been "moralized"—interpreted allegorically to illustrate philosophical truths. This tradition was demonstrably fading in Marlowe's day, but his version of the *Amores* gives no hint that the tradition had ever even existed.[3]

Indeed, the poem is almost unElizabethan in its lack of sententia. Later, when Marlowe wrote *Hero and Leander,* he ironically attached conventional tags throughout the story, but no moral tags illuminate the *Elegies.*

In fact, the *Elegies* are altogether unconcerned with ideas, and this is astonishing. Marlowe's plays are marked by intellectual conflict, and he seems in them to be a passionate inquirer into first principles. Perhaps this critical temper grew from his training in Classical dialectic and in the abstract ratiocination to which Cambridge was devoted. But the *Elegies* lack evidence of philosophical restlessness. As Una Ellis-Fermor says, "the country into which they lead him is untouched by that fine, clear wind of thought."[4] Not only did Marlowe accept the physical world for what it was, asking no questions, he also translated the unintellectual Ovid line by line, and he followed without criticism the mistakes of his sixteenth-century Latin editions as dutifully as he followed their felicities, even when the resulting lines turned out to be meaningless.[5] What he produced is sometimes turgid, sometimes opaque; but, remarkably enough, it is almost purely Ovidian. These *Elegies,* like Ovid's *Amores,* exist in a charming world of color and physical beauty, unencumbered by conscience, unburdened by guilt. Less urbane than the original because more monotonous—Marlowe was just learning his craft —the translation occasionally achieves a line worthy of his greatest days. In all this mediocrity, we occasionally catch a glimpse of things to come.

If Marlowe is not yet in full control of his poetic instrument, he gives promise of what Jonson was to call his "mighty line":[6]

> What helps it me of fierce Achill to sing?
> What good to me will either Ajax bring?
> Or he who warr'd and wander'd twenty year?
> Or woeful Hector whom wild jades did tear?
> (II.i. 29–32)

We also glimpse the future interest in geographic space and material richness:

> Now o'er the sea from her old love comes she
> That draws the day from heaven's cold axle-tree.
> Aurora, whither slidest thou? . . .

[28]

Whither runn'st thou, that men and women love not?
Hold in thy rosy horses that they move not.
                                        (I.xiii. 1–3, 9–10)

And, now and then, Marlowe even rises to eloquence:

Therefore when flint and iron wear away,
Verse is immortal and shall n'er decay.
To verse let kings place, and kingly shows,
And banks o'er which gold-bearing Tagus flows.
Let base-conceited wits admire vile things,
Fair Phoebus lead me to the Muses' springs.
About my head be quivering myrtle wound,
And in sad lovers' heads let me be found.
The living, not the dead, can envy bite,
For after death all men receive their right.
Then though death rakes my bones in funeral fire,
I'll live, and as he pulls me down mount higher.
                                        (I.xv. 31–42)

If, in the translation from Ovid, we see the sensual side of Marlowe's nature, in the translation from Lucan we see another side, his interest in war. Generally thought to have been made shortly after the Ovid while he was still at Cambridge, the *Civil Wars* was not published until 1600. John Wolf entered it and *Hero and Leander* in the Stationers' Register on September 28, 1593, only a few months after Marlowe's death at Deptford. Tucker Brooke has guessed that Wolf intended to publish the two works together, presumably to cash in on Marlowe's notorious end.[7] If such were the plan, nothing came of it. The poems appeared individually, several years later: *Hero and Leander* in 1598; Marlowe's translation of Lucan's *Civil Wars* in 1600.

Lucan's epic concerns the civil war between Caesar and the Roman Senate, and it was left unfinished when Lucan died at age twenty-six. Inappropriately but traditionally referred to as the *Pharsalia*—the title refers to events only in one book, the seventh—the *Civil Wars* is distinctly a minor work of Lucan's, sophisticated, verbose, and static. Abounding in apostrophe and all kinds of literary figures, it contains no subtle rhythms. It is poetically monotonous, however extravagant rhetorically. Because the style is so artificial, Quintilian thought Lucan a better model for orators than for poets;[8] but Marlowe has yet another interest in this elaborate account of Roman strife. Under his hand Lucan's *Civil Wars* loses much of its verbal finish—the subject matter, not the language, attracted him. Because he sympathized with Lucan's desire to make the flesh crawl, the translation points ahead to *Tamburlaine*, not back to Classical oratory. Marlowe responded to Lucan's Caesarism, not to his hyperbole.

Like the Ovid before it, the Lucan is a line-by-line translation; but unlike the Ovid it is blank verse. Though an apprentice piece, it is more accomplished than the Ovid. Where the original Latin sentences are involuted and intricate, Marlowe's English is relatively simple. Marlowe's narrative movement is direct, and his lines are usually straightforward, however twisted individual passages may be. Where there are ambiguities, the fault is more often Lucan's than Marlowe's; and most people would prefer his version to the original. Lucan's material and manner are "Englished"—but more, they become Marlovian. The invocation to Caesar as emperor is completely in Marlowe's manner:

> . . . thou wilt reign as king,
> Or mount the Sun's flame-bearing chariot,
> And with bright restless fire compass the earth,
> Undaunted though her former guide be chang'd;
> Nature and every power shall give thee place,
> What god it please thee be, or where to sway. (47–52)

The Roman Caesar has become an Elizabethan tyrant, complete with restless fire, plume-bearing chariot, and god-defying ambition. Moreover, it is worth noting that Caesar's speeches lack the irony which Quintilian praised. They contain instead some measure of bravura, as when Caesar says:

> An end of peace; here end polluted laws;
> Hence, leagues and covenants; Fortune, thee I follow,
> War and the Destinies shall try my cause. (227–29)

He sounds like Mortimer Junior in *Edward II* who expresses similar sentiments in similar words.

The Roman crowds succumb to the conquering hero without battle, even as the tributary kings fall down before Tamburlaine; and Caesar's generals are as enchanted by their leader as Tamburlaine's. The chief centurion says to him: "Love over-rules my will, I must obey thee," and he continues:

> . . . should'st thou bid me
> Entomb my sword within my brother's bowels,
> Or father's throat, or women's groaning womb,
> This hand (albeit unwilling) should perform it;
> Or rob the gods, or sacred temples fire . . .
>
> (373, 376–80)

Unnatural marvels foretell Caesar's approach to Rome, but they are what one might expect in such a poem dealing with such a hero. The "saints and household-gods/ Sweat tears" and "ominous birds/ Defil'd the day." Wild beasts are seen at night "leaving the woods" to "lodge in the streets of Rome"; cattle mutter in human speech (554 ff); for nature reflects the ambitions of men. In this poem the grandeur of events and the glamour of battles fascinate Marlowe. This is a young man's ecstatic response to violence, danger, and charismatic leadership. Marlowe found in Lucan a universe which responded to the determination of great men, one which yielded to power; for in *Pharsalia* the heroes exist in a world of their own making.

And yet certain qualities of Lucan's rhetoric influence Marlowe's later work. His elaborate accounts of religious events reinforced Marlowe's Renaissance taste for pageants. Marlowe includes Lucan's account of Roman color and noise and auguries even though the symbolic significance of the spectacles is silently passed over. What was literary for Lucan becomes physical for Marlowe. Lucan's roll of proper names appeals to his senses; for although the identity of Lucan's persons and places must have been obscure to Marlowe, in combination they fire his imagination, which loved to dwell on the remote. As in his later work, these exotic names stretch the margins of his vision.

But we must not overpraise the translation; it is journeyman work. Spenser learned his art by translating Petrarch and Du-Bellay before striking out on his own; and Sidney asserted in his *Apologie for Poesie* (*ca.* 1580) that though poets are born, yet they must learn their craft by imitation. In this tradition Marlowe turned into English a Latin epic of violent civil war. No story-teller and no accurate historian, Lucan is always forceful; and his violence held Marlowe through seven hundred lines of difficult, sometimes impenetrable, Latin. As we have noted, Marlowe, in choosing to translate Ovid, showed his sensitivity to the sensual world; in translating Lucan, he showed his fascination with violent power. These remained his interests until his death.

II *The First Play*

The Tragedy of Dido, Queen of Carthage, as D. C. Allen has stated, "does not move in the thundering realms of the universal absolutes" like Marlowe's great plays;[9] but, like the poems, it demands our attention for historical reasons and in its own right. In the opinion of most scholars *Dido* was written during Marlowe's Cambridge years, after the translations of Lucan and Ovid, and it shows a certain mastery of verse and considerably greater freedom from its Classical sources than the poems. The title page of its only surviving edition (1594) says it was "played by the Children of Her Majesty's Chapel," presumably when these young players visited Ipswich near Cambridge in 1586-87; but there is no record that *Dido* was ever acted in London. Thomas Nashe, a younger colleague of Marlowe's at Cambridge and later one of the "University Wits" who tried to eke out a journalist's living in London, is named on the 1594 title page as co-author of the play. His part in it must have been small, judging from the style of the piece. Perhaps he touched up the text after 1590, before it was published; but there is no evidence for this supposition. It seems wisest to assume that Marlowe wrote all the play early in his career and that Nashe's name is more or less gratuitously attached.

As before, Marlowe drew his material from the Latin Classics, this time from Virgil. Drawing on the first, second, and fourth books of the *Aeneid,* Marlowe made several significant modifications of the epic. The opening scene, for example, consists of a most unVirgilian dialogue between Jupiter and Ganymede, "the female wanton boy" as Venus refers to him. When the scene opens, Jupiter is "dandling Ganymede upon his knee," suing him for his love. Ganymede rather petulantly, even vindictively, resists him; and, before the episode is concluded, Jupiter has given him "These linkèd gems [which] My Juno ware upon her marriage day" (I.i. 42-3). Obviously, their relationship is neither godlike nor dignified. Shortly Venus upbraids

Jupiter, not for his infidelity to Juno but for his negligence of her mortal son Aeneas:

> False Jupiter, reward'st thou virtue so?
> What, is not piety exempt from woe?
> Then die Aeneas in thine innocence,
> Since that religion hath no recompense. (I.i. 78–81)

The gods seem a frivolous lot, and indeed mythology portrays them as such, but from the first scene it is clear that *Dido, Queen of Carthage* was not written by a pious man.

In this first scene Marlowe has introduced two ideas which are to appear and reappear throughout this and all his plays: gods are frivolous; men are noble. In *Dido* we are early struck by the dignity of the mortals—compared to them, the gods are anything but supremely admirable. Not only Jupiter but Venus is belittled; at best she is maternal, and she is never captivating. Greeting her shipwrecked son Aeneas, she shows a grandmotherly affection for his son Ascanius, and she even sings him lullabies (II.i. 334ff). When she and Juno meet, they engage in the kind of female tussle that one sees in the farmyard of *Gammer Gurton's Needle* (III.ii). Marlowe seems bent on depreciating her immortal charm. As for Cupid—he is hardly more than a spoiled child selling his coy offerings at the highest rate, rather like any pampered son of doting parents. Throughout the play the gods are self-indulgent and seem unworthy of human sacrifices. They teeter constantly on the edge of the ludicrous, inspiring in us something close to contemptuous laughter. If these gods have charge of the affairs of men, Marlowe implies, men had best look to their own welfare; "religion hath no recompense" (I.i. 81).

Happily, the human beings in the play are not totally dependent on these silly gods. From our first meeting with Aeneas, we know that a power other than that of the gods exists in the world of this play: that of Aeneas himself. Achates, Aeneas' companion, gives the clue:

> Brave prince of Troy, thou only art our god,
> That by thy virtues free'st us from annoy,
> And makes our hopes survive to coming joys.
> Do thou but smile and cloudy heaven will clear,
> Whose night and day descendeth from thy brows.
> (I.i. 152–56)

That the gods can be of some help to this paragon of leadership, there can be no doubt; and, conversely, they can destroy him. But from the first Aeneas is more forceful and more direct than they. Fortune awaits on him, Venus tells us and him:

> Fortune hath favored thee, whate'er thou be.
> . . . .
> And so I leave thee to thy fortune's lot,
> Wishing good luck unto thy wandering steps.
> (I.i. 231, 238–39)

The *fortune* to which Venus refers, under whose aegis Aeneas clearly stands, is not the medieval Dame Fortuna who teaches humility before the vicissitudes of life. This Fortuna is not the instructress in *contemptu mundi;* she is scarcely more than luck. Aeneas is one of those favored mortals to whom men and gods alike pay respect. If he does not with his own hand turn Fortune's wheel about and if he does not hold Fortune bound fast in iron chains, as Tamburlaine does (I.iii. 173–4), Aeneas is nonetheless a man with whom to reckon. The gods are no match for him, in valor or purpose or eloquence.

Aeneas' long account to Dido of the fall of Troy illustrates the relative parts that gods and men play in worldly affairs. According to Virgil (Book II), Troy fell because the gods aided the Greeks. The Trojan horse was contrived with Pallas' help, and Aeneas escaped the burning city when the gods willed it. He was guided constantly by the omens they sent. Virgil's epic action takes place on a cosmic stage; but Marlowe's is much smaller; and his Aeneas occupies a different world—essentially a petty and even malicious one. Old Priamus, king of Troy, is murdered on the altar of Jove, where we would have expected him to be protected. He pleads with his attacker, the young Pyrrhus:

> . . . remember what I was,
> Father of fifty sons, but they are slain;
> Lord of my fortune, but my fortune's turned. . . .
> (II.i. 233–35)

Priamus is less the victim of the gods' anger than of capricious circumstance. Marlowe's gods have not abdicated; they are just irresponsible.

The account of the fall of Troy is one of the high points

of the play; not so magnificent as Virgil's, it is yet exciting, and its tone is rather unsettling. In Virgil we give our undivided admiration to Aeneas as he flees burning Troy, directed by the gods. He carries his aged father on his back and draws his young son along by the hand. When his wife, who follows close behind, is lost, he returns to the burning city to find her; and he only gives up the search when her ghost instructs him to depart. Marlowe reduces this moving episode to half a line: "O there I lost my wife . . . ," Aeneas says (II.i. 270). We might forgive Aeneas' callousness—remembering that Marlowe has only one hundred and eighty lines to tell a story on which Virgil expended eight hundred—but his desertion of his sister Cassandra, whom he leaves "sprawling in the streets" (II.i. 274), seems equally unfeeling. And his insensitive account of the death of old Priam, ripped "from the navel to the throat at once. . ." (II.i. 255–56), was glanced at, indeed almost burlesqued, by the Player in *Hamlet* (II.ii. 499ff).

Considering all the passages about Aeneas, we have difficulty making out how we ought to react to Marlowe's characterization. He does not measure up to the grandeur of Virgil's hero; and many details of his speech and action, taken in isolation, make him almost contemptible. Still, the other characters—and Marlowe—give him their admiration. We must conclude that Marlowe in *Dido* was not yet firmly in control of his medium, not capable of fully executing his dramatic plans. Aeneas is conceived in monumental size, but he is inconsistently realized. The youthful discrepancy between aspiration and achievement makes this play essentially an apprentice piece.[10]

This is not meant to imply, however, that *Dido, Queen of Carthage* does not have its dramatic moments, for even the apprentice Marlowe had genius. Immediately following Aeneas' account of the fall of Troy, for instance, he has written a sharply contrasting scene which makes a very neat point (II.i. 304–39). Aeneas has been describing the death of noble warriors, but this description is followed by an episode concerned with willful children. In it Venus bribes the child Ascanius with sugar-almonds, sweet conserves, and a quiver and bow. Critics have commented on the similarity of the lyric verse in this scene to the fairy scenes in Shakespeare's *A Midsummer Night's Dream*.[11]

What they have not observed is how similar in size and consequence Venus and Jupiter are to Titania and Oberon. In Shakespeare's play, the fairies seem the more exquisite by being
contrasted to Bottom and the mechanics. In Marlowe's play,
Venus and Cupid are the pettier in being contrasted to the thunder of falling Troy. By this careful juxtaposition of action, Marlowe disparages the gods once more and elevates human achievement.

Nor is Aeneas, for all his inconsistencies, the only considerable figure of this play. Dido is really its protagonist, and on her
Marlowe expends his talent. An Amazon, she built Carthage
and, like Queen Elizabeth, has refused mighty kings for con-
sorts. She understands her own authority:

> Those that dislike what Dido gives in charge,
> Command my guard to slay for their offence.
> Shall vulgar peasants storm at what I do?
> The ground is mine that gives them sustenance,
> The air wherein they breathe, the water, fire,
> All that they have, their lands, their goods, their lives;
> And I, the goddess of all these. . .   (IV.iv. 71–77)

Dido is a female Tamburlaine; braving the gods out of their
heavens, she asserts her authority as a goddess on earth. She
is a fit match for Aeneas and partakes with him of Caesarism.
When she is deserted by Aeneas, she rises, like Cleopatra, to a
worthy eloquence; and, again like Cleopatra, she kills herself.
Her self-immolation is a gesture of great audacity. Tricked into
loving Aeneas, she can at least control her death. Like other
Marlowe protagonists, she is too great for the role in which she
has been cast; and she breaks out of her mortal limitations.

In his outline, Marlowe is successful with Dido—as he is,
generally, with Aeneas. Even so, some of Dido's most important
scenes are puzzling, largely because of Marlowe's dramaturgical
ineptness. The first of these is that in which Cupid, masquerad-
ing as Ascanius, injures Dido with his arrow, causing her to
fall in love with Aeneas. Just a moment before, Iarbas had been
pleading for her hand. "Fear not, Iarbas" she had told him;
"Dido may be thine" (III.i. 19). After she has been infected by
Cupid, she seems unable either to reject Iarbas or to accept

Aeneas. She contradicts herself irresolutely. The scene has been called comic,[12] but I think Marlowe is reaching for more than laughter: He is trying to dramatize the conflict in Dido's mind between the legitimate love which she may feel for Iarbas and the destructive passion for Aeneas which has been inspired by Cupid. Marlowe wants to show Dido's reason in active conflict with her passion, but he does not yet have the dramatic means. Like his fellow playwrights—Greene, Peele, Kyd, and even Shakespeare—Marlowe is searching for a nonallegorical means of representing the interior life. In his short career he was able to achieve it most fully and consistently only in his late play, *Edward II;* but by that time he had Shakespeare for a model.[13] In this early play, he stumbles.

The climactic scenes in which Aeneas decides to desert Dido have caused some comment. Their seeming inconsistencies can be resolved by recognizing that Marlowe attempts in them to show interior conflict similar to that seen a moment before with Dido. In Act III, scene iv, Dido and Aeneas declare their love for each other and promise eternal fidelity, though such declarations do not come easily to either of them. Early in the scene Aeneas observes that they two have met by chance as Venus and Mars met, and Dido answers: "Why, that was in a net, where we are loose./ And yet I am not free. O, would I were!" (III.iv. 4-5). Dido must be both queen—the commander of all her people—and woman—the patient receiver of Aeneas' love. Here in the cave of love with fewer misgivings than she, Aeneas swears "Never to like or love any but her" (III.iv. 50). The scene ends when Dido gives Aeneas bracelets and the wedding ring "Wherewith my husband wooed me yet a maid" (III.iv. 62). We are reminded that Jupiter gave Ganymede the jewels worn by Juno on her wedding day, and the relationship of Aeneas and Dido is defined for us: theirs is an illicit passion. But the dignity of the human lovers is heightened by its contrast with Jupiter's lack of dignity with Ganymede. The mortals feel themselves bound by a code higher than the gods' code. They are not free to indulge their appetites as the gods seem to be. In short, they are ethically superior to their superiors.

The division between passion and responsibility is immediately reiterated. As Enobarbus is able to describe Cleopatra and define the lustfulness of her liaison with Antony, so Achates identifies the relationship between Dido and Aeneas:

> . . . Can heaven endure this sight?
> Iarbas, curse that unrevenging Jove,
> Whose flinty darts slept in Typhoeus' den,
> Whiles these adulterers surfeited with sin.
> (IV.i. 17–20)

Shortly he urges Aeneas to desert Carthage for his destiny in Italy, and Aeneas replies: "I fain would go, yet beauty calls me back" (IV.iii. 46). Aeneas, like Antony, says to his mistress: "When I leave thee, death be my punishment" (IV.iv. 56). At first blush Marlowe's Aeneas seems to be vacillating, in a way foreign to Virgil's Aeneas. But he is not. We are not to understand him as weak, for Marlowe is striving to represent the double nature of Aeneas, the conflicting attractions of Dido and Rome. We are invited to consider interior discord in Aeneas as we have earlier seen it in Dido.

Marlowe is not content to represent the conflict of love in his principal characters only. He gives a comic representation of it in the scene between the Nurse and Cupid. Cupid, held in the Nurse's arms, wounds the ancient woman, and she thereupon yearns for love, toothless as she is. Tucker Brooke asks us to compare this scene, in which "the Nurse's mind chops about from one extreme to the other," with Dido's irresolution upon being wounded by Cupid's arrow. And Brooke concludes that "Evidently the author had little skill in feminine psychology."[14] Marlowe may have had little skill in feminine psychology, but his problem at the moment is more general: he seems unable to represent persuasively the rival considerations in the problem of choice. Here he tries to treat comically what he elsewhere treats tragically. Marlowe is not able to represent the rival claims, but we can see what he is aiming at.

Dido, Queen of Carthage is the only play in which Marlowe dealt with romantic love as a major human motivation. Wherever love appears in his other plays, it is of subordinate concern. Love does not drive Tamburlaine to great conquest; it is his reward after battle. Love does not comfort Edward II; his attachment to Gaveston is only one aspect of his self-indulgence. And for

Doctor Faustus, love is replaced by lust. Marlowe thought love disruptive: it diverts Dido from her responsibilities as queen, and it nearly keeps Aeneas from reaching Italy. Irrational, it comes unbidden; and, like disease, it can hardly be controlled by the will. Its end is nearly always fatal. Dido kills herself for love; and Anna, her sister, similarly kills herself. Indeed, Anna's suicide follows so closely upon Dido's that it is almost funny—Marlowe is here guilty of a dramatic miscalculation. But her death nonetheless reinforces Marlowe's view of the destructive power of love.

Only Aeneas escapes destroying love, but he is driven by his destiny. Worldly ambition claims his allegiance, just as worldly aspiration inspires all Marlowe's protagonists. *Dido* differs from the other plays by claiming a major interest in a suffering woman rather than in an ambitious man. Otherwise it contains Marlowe's favorite ideas: the attractions of power, the ineffectualness of the gods, the nobility of men, the fascination of the sensual world. And, like the other plays, it lacks a sympathy with charitable emotions.

III   *The End of the Beginning*

Dido, Queen of Carthage is the kind of play that a young translator of Ovid and Lucan might be expected to write. Its subject is erotic love, Ovid's theme. The licentiousness of love is dealt with more summarily in the play than in the poem, for Ovid was too rich for stage representation in 1586 or 1587. *Dido* is also concerned with power, Lucan's theme, and in two different ways. Marlowe's Aeneas is the first of the supermen who seem driven by fate to godlike authority; as such, he is a predecessor of Tamburlaine. In addition, this play may well represent a different aspect of Marlowe's interest in power; it appears to have been his personal bid for place in the Elizabethan court. By 1587 he had had some experience with power by way of backstairs espionage. His mysterious dealings with the Walsinghams and Lord Burghley introduced him to the great world, and he was to have more dealings later. His appetite was whetted. Some years before, John Lyly, a young Oxford graduate, had set court fashion with his *Euphues* (1579) and then had attempted to capitalize on this success with court comedies. These charming prose pieces, written for child actors, were Lyly's bid for patronage. In 1586 it was still too soon for Marlowe to see that these were not going to succeed, and they may have seemed a new means of approaching the court.[15] At Cambridge, Marlowe hastily wrote a play much like Lyly's. Like Lyly's plays, *Dido, Queen of Carthage* was acted by a children's company. Like them, it dealt with amorous intrigues, suffering lovers, courtly compliment, Classical story, and mythological settings— all in a high and artful language.

But Marlowe went Lyly one better. Both his ambitions and his talents were greater than Lyly's. His play was a tragedy and therefore more serious; his language was poetry and therefore more admirable; and his subject was epic and therefore more awesome. Marlowe sought more than Lyly's drawing room authority; with this play, he may have aspired to enter the circles of real power. It did not, of course, accomplish its purposes. Nobody paid any attention whatsoever to *Dido, Queen of Carthage,* and thereafter in London Marlowe turned his attention to the public rather than to the court theater.

By the spring of 1587 Marlowe had long since given up any expectation of a career in the Church. Now he gave his admiration to heroes, not gods. An intellectual and an iconoclast, he strove to call all the old affirmations into question. When he left Cambridge, power seemingly remained his overriding interest, for it was the subject of the plays that established him as a maker of English literature. Once in London, he may never have looked at *Dido, Queen of Carthage* again; as we have noted, it was only published after his death when an enterprising printer attempted to cash in on the scandals associated with Marlowe's name. From every point of view, this first venture into the great world of fame and power was unsuccessful. The next was not.

CHAPTER 3

Caesarism:
Tamburlaine the Great

I *The* Tamburlaine *Problems*

WHEN MARLOWE left Cambridge in the spring of 1587 for a career in London, he had a few friends in high places, a restless talent ready for exercise, and a draft of *Tamburlaine the Great*. With this play he made a permanent mark on the English stage. It was, of course, a popular success; but, more important, it eventually helped determine the idiom of dramatic speech in the period of English drama's greatest brilliance. Marlowe had the genius to recognize the importance of his innovations, for his Prologue begins: "From jigging veins of rhyming mother wits,/ And such conceits as clownage keeps in pay,/ We'll lead you to the stately tent of war . . ." (1-3). The English theater had reached a turning point and was henceforth to be profoundly different from what it had been before. No longer would it be halting and didactic; now it was to be eloquent, sophisticated, and, at its best, philosophical. From his first lines Marlowe was self-consciously revolutionary. Now nearly three centuries later we may not always feel the audacity of this extraordinary play, but we must recognize that it was a major event in the establishment of the new drama.

Tamburlaine the Great was so successful that a second Tamburlaine play was quickly called for. The Prologue to *Tamburlaine the Great, Part Two* refers to "the general welcomes" which "hath made our poet pen his second Part." It was probably written in 1587 and acted immediately.[1] The public did not quickly forget either of these companion plays, and references to them are almost innumerable during the next three generations.[2] Entered in the Stationers' Register in August, 1590, the two parts were issued together that year, and by 1606 three more editions had followed. None contained Marlowe's name on the title page, but his authorship has been accepted on both stylistic and historical grounds. The relative excellence of the 1590 edition suggests that Marlowe himself had some hand in seeing it through the press. It was the only work of his published during his brief lifetime.

The two plays have considerably more than historical interest. *Tamburlaine* does not reach the profundity of *Doctor Faustus,* or the sophistication of *Edward II,* but it is eloquent and, as one of its recent critics has said, this is "the most solid and unflawed of Marlowe's plays."[3] The *Tamburlaine* plays are animated by a controlling concept which unifies their varied incidents and their extravagant language. Far from being "clumsy and jerky,"[4] their episodic structure is suited to their theme, as we will see, and their rhetoric, which to some sounds like "rant and bombast,"[5] is essential to their high artifice. Marlowe "was writing in passion of a man of passion, and his figures are those of passion," F. P. Wilson has said.[6] Marlowe is not trying to give a recognizable picture of ordinary experience in *Tamburlaine*; he is not interested in anatomizing the developing of human beings, nor is he providing an exposition of Tudor political theory as Shakespeare's history plays are now so often assumed to do.

We cannot discover the will of God working through the affairs of state in these two plays; indeed, they contain a "strong and direct denial of the role of providence in human affairs."[7] Instead of traditional conclusions like those of the morality writers whom he abuses as those "rhyming mother wits," Marlowe dramatizes his sharply individual understanding of man's relationship to the universe. He was an intellectual unfettered by orthodoxy, but he and the morality writers were alike at least in that they both tackled philosophical problems. As Professor Clemen says, "the focal point of the play is an idea" (p. 113). If Marlowe's brilliant dramatic language, his rhetoric, fascinates us first, his ideas give the play importance.

Marlowe in some respects is rather like Milton.[8] Ever since William Blake, critics of *Paradise Lost* have struggled against the assumption that Milton was of Satan's party without knowing it. The rebellion of Lucifer has had a charm for Romantic and post-Romantic readers that has nearly alienated us from Milton's epic. Marlowe, two generations before Milton, dramatized the satanic hero with which *Paradise Lost* is credited. Tamburlaine and Lucifer are cut from the same cloth, but Marlowe, unlike Milton, can be seen as knowingly and willfully of Satan's party.

Tamburlaine is the first full scale portrait of the attractively diabolical; he is the first Romantic rebel. Cruel beyond belief, bloody beyond comprehension, violent to the point of irrationality, he is also spellbinding, in part because he is so cruel, so bloody, and so violent. Marlowe's great accomplishment is that he makes the diabolical attractive without glossing over its essentially infernal nature. In Tamburlaine, Marlowe gives dramatic credit to all the base inclinations which civilization seeks to restrain. And, when Tamburlaine takes us back to the jungle, we exult. The play asks us to take pleasure in the irrational, in the barbaric, and is not the less important for that. *Tamburlaine* is anti-Christian.[9] The questions we must ask about the play are two: Is Tamburlaine as spellbinding as here asserted? And, second, if so, how does Marlowe persuade us to accept the unqualifiedly diabolical as heroic? The answers can be reached by a detailed examination of the structure of the plays.

II Tamburlaine, *Part One*

The Prologue to *Tamburlaine, Part One* suggests what our attitude toward Tamburlaine ought to be. This "Scythian Tamburlaine/Threat'ning the world with high astounding terms" (Prol. 4–5) deserves our admiration, we learn. No opprobrium can be detected in the Prologue and we are asked to acknowledge Tamburlaine's glory.

The high praise with which the play begins is continued

through the three general movements of the play that follow. In the first movement—Acts I and II—Tamburlaine looms tall by standing next to midgets; Marlowe juxtaposes speeches, characters, and scenes for dramatic effect. In the second movement—Act III—he is shown to be less barbarous than Bajazeth and Zabina, the representatives of the Turkish civilization which he overcomes. Tamburlaine's violence is less objectionable than the Turks'. In the third movement of the play—Acts IV and V—we see Tamburlaine usurp Jove's throne of power; he openly defies Christian law and ordinary human sympathy. Out of context, the various episodes of conquest would repulse us; but as arranged in the play they never alienate us from the conqueror. To see how this is managed, it is wisest to examine *Tamburlaine* as it comes to us in sequence, on the stage, observing Marlowe's dramaturgy scene by scene.

After the Prologue, Tamburlaine, the Scythian shepherd, is not immediately brought on stage—his merit is so great that his entrance must be carefully prepared. King Mycetes of Persia and his brother are introduced first so that their relative pettiness may heighten Tamburlaine's magnificence. Mycetes is nearly a caricature of the vacillating king. Not so obtuse as to miss the rather crude innuendos of his inferiors, he is yet too indecisive and too weak to correct them. He is the butt of crude joking (I.i. 97–98) which no doubt brought down the house. Mycetes plays at being king, strikes postures which he thinks appropriate to his place, and mouths clichés uncritically. When he sends Theridamas to defeat Tamburlaine, for example, he says: "Return with speed; time passeth swift away./ Our life is frail, and we may die today" (I.i. 67–68). The emptiness of Mycetes' *memento mori* tag is underscored by his next speech, in which he talks of his "milk-white steeds. . . All loaden with the heads of killèd men" (76–77). Mycetes' contemptible weakness disposes us to favor any challenger—Tamburlaine included. The play begins, therefore, in a low key from which Tamburlaine's grandeur may rise, splendidly.

Cosroe, Mycetes' brother, also prepares for Tamburlaine, but in a different way. Plotting to grasp the crown from Mycetes, he receives the homage of all the vassal states of Persia who "invest your highness emperor"; and we see that Cosroe is more fitted to rule than his brother. His ascent to the throne is as little revolutionary as any regal usurpation can be. In these opening lines of the play, we agree with Ortygius that the nation and its honor require that Cosroe "reign sole king." By the end of the first scene, we are convinced that the silly Mycetes ought to give way to his politic brother who is next in royal succession. Marlowe has carefully set the stage for his hero's first appearance.

When Tamburlaine makes his entrance, legitimacy becomes a schoolmaster's petty consideration. From the very first we see that Tamburlaine, "a shepherd by my parentage" (I.ii. 35), does not live by the laws which bind lesser men, even kings. Greater than others, he will be ruled by laws appropriate to himself alone. When he throws off his shepherd's weeds to reveal his armor and when he declares his intention "to be a terror to the world" (I.ii. 38), we see that ordinary standards of judgment must be passed over. His speeches, which define his nature, are filled with allusions to the rebels of Classical legend; and his imagery, as Professor Clemen has noted, is that of wish fulfillment (p. 119). He is obsessed with himself, and the torrents of his language overwhelm both opponents who resist him and aides who encourage him.

Even those speeches occasioned by his love for Zenocrate, the captive princess, are really addressed to nobody. They have a rhetorical rather than a narrative function. Zenocrate's six-line assertion of herself, for example, is not so much answered as engulfed by Tamburlaine's glorious twenty-five line reply beginning:

> Zenocrate, lovelier than the love of Jove,
> Brighter than is the silver Rhodope,
> Fairer than whitest snow on Scythian hills,
> Thy person is more worth to Tamburlaine
> Than the possession of the Persian crown,
> Which gracious stars have promised at my birth.
> (I.ii. 87–92)

The passage does not describe Zenocrate; it illuminates Tamburlaine's aspirations. Throughout this whole scene, and indeed the whole play, he is drunk with his awareness of himself:

> I hold the Fates bound fast in iron chains,

And with my hand turn Fortune's wheel about,
And sooner shall the sun fall from his sphere
Then Tamburlaine be slain or overcome.
(I.ii. 173–76)

When he claims that Zenocrate is more valuable to him than the Persian crown, we do not believe him. His language consistently associates her with booty. He values conquest—and her as part of it. The expectation of world conquest inspires him to the greatest flights of imagination. His bejeweled language blinds us.

We are so blinded that we cannot resist the man who speaks in so glorious a fashion. We are not asked to consider how such a being came to be, nor how he is able to realize his ambitions; we can only accept him and them. Theridamas, sent by the king of Persia, expects to resist the Scythian's aspirations; but, like us, he is "enchanted" and "won with [his] words and conquered with [his] looks" (I.ii. 227). If Tamburlaine has no claim to the thrones he proposes to occupy, we do not boggle at that. He is born with majesty and "sleep'st every night with conquest on [his] brows" (V.ii. 296). The first act of the play places the dramatic issue before us: kings who rule by right of law are faced down by this creature who rules by right of power. Our sympathies are totally with the revolutionary, in part because Mycetes and Cosroe are naïve and ineffectual, but more because the usurper is hypnotically attractive. And, step by step, as we discover where such attraction takes us, we see that even violent cruelty cannot estrange us. Paradoxically, his cruelty remains part of his fascination.

In Act I, Mycetes was subjected to laughter; in Act II he is made even more ludicrous. When symbolically he hides his crown in "a goodly stratagem" (II.iv. 11), Tamburlaine refuses to snatch it from him, nor will he bargain for it. He asserts that he will take it by force of arms alone. In this act Cosroe, who is also made ridiculous, but more subtly, plots to use Tamburlaine for his own purposes. Not realizing what manner of superman he deals with, he wants to make the Scythian shepherd his regent-king, but we have seen Tamburlaine with Theridamas and know that he can be no man's lieutenant. When Cosroe says, "Thee do I make my regent of Persia/ And general lieutenant of my armies" (II.v. 8–9), we await the flexing of the giant's muscles. When Tamburlaine breaks his imaginary legal bonds, we exult with him. His sudden recognition of his strength is one of the great moments of the play, and the combination of rhetorical questions and exotic names characterizes Marlowe's style:

> Is it not brave to be a king, Techelles?
> Usumcasane and Theridamas,
> Is it not passing brave to be a king
> And ride in triumph through Persepolis?
>   (II.v. 51–54)

Limitless horizons stretch before Tamburlaine, for only the strutting Cosroe stands between them and him. He will take the Persian crown: " 'Twill prove a pretty jest, in faith, my friends" (II.v. 90), he says. Conquest is sport, and war a joyous game; and this delight contrasts with Cosroe's legalistic anger: "What means this devilish shepherd to aspire/ With such a giantly presumption. . ." (II.vi. 1–2). Tamburlaine's justification for conquest is implied long before he states it: his strength.

Cosroe's scheming legalism has been explicitly compared to Tamburlaine's straightforward action, and our sympathy has been carefully directed to Tamburlaine. The usurper has gaiety, admiring friends, and power. He is not Machiavellian, as has been said.[10] He is in fact almost anti-intellectual; for it is Marlowe, not Tamburlaine, who has the philosophical mind. Cosroe plots, not Tamburlaine; Mycetes praises poetry, not Tamburlaine (II.iii. 54ff); and Tamburlaine's famous apostrophe to beauty (V.ii. 96ff) subordinates esthetic to warlike values. War and action, not art and thought—these earn his commendation. Tamburlaine never plans beyond the battle before him; and, ironically, he does not recognize his full strength as quickly as others do. He may have the Fates bound fast in iron chains, but he does not identify his fated goals until they are upon him. Possessed by a blind ambition, he is driven independent of any will of his own; and his celebrated apologia justifies conquest more than it initiates it:

> Nature, that framed us of four elements
> Warring within our breasts for regiment,

Doth teach us all to have aspiring minds.
Our souls, whose faculties can comprehend
The wondrous architecture of the world
And measure every wandering planet's course,
Still climbing after knowledge infinite,
And always moving as the restless spheres,
Wills us to wear ourselves and never rest,
Until we reach the ripest fruit of all,
That perfect bliss and sole felicity,
The sweet fruition of an earthly crown.   (II.vii. 18–29)

Tamburlaine finds a precedent for his revolutionary aspiration in Jove himself. Overcome by Tamburlaine's elemental force, Cosroe dies, implying by his death that resistance to Tamburlaine exhausts the disbeliever. His dying curse is not taken seriously by anybody, including us; and Act II ends with the new emperor of Persia more secure "Than if the gods had held a parliament,/ And all pronounced me king of Persia" (II.vii. 66–67).

The first movement of the play is now complete. In it, we have seen that Tamburlaine is an irresistible conqueror, a revolutionary who overturns established orders through the authority of his person. Although Cosroe has declared him "barbarous and bloody," his only barbarity thus far is his disrespect for legitimacy, and his only violence has been offstage. The objections to Tamburlaine's action have been carefully stated, but they have been ridiculed. We are firmly of his party; and through the next scenes, which deal with the conquest of Bajazeth—this second movement of the play, which extends through Act III— we continue our allegiance to him.

In overcoming Mycetes and Cosroe, Tamburlaine had met no real match. Bajazeth, emperor of the Turks, who is more than a cut above them, sees himself as a kind of African Tamburlaine, invincible and famous. He, like Tamburlaine, is contemptuous of opponents and confident of his mighty arms; and his voice is full of Tamburlaine's kind of bravado, as he says: "And all the trees are blasted with our breaths" (III.i. 55). In his first scene with Tamburlaine, we see in him other qualities which Tamburlaine shortly assumes. Bajazeth is extravagantly bloody and much more violent than Tamburlaine has seemed to be. It is he who says "Let thousands die! Their slaughtered carcasses/ Shall serve for walls and bulwarks to the rest" (III.iii. 138–39); and it is he who thirsts "to drink the feeble Persians' blood" (III.iii. 165).

Moreover, Bajazeth and his queen, Zabina, propose the cruel punishments which Tamburlaine later imposes. They suggest that defeated kings draw the conqueror's chariot (III.iii. 79–80) and that captive queens deserve to be servants to servants: "Thou shalt be laundress to my waiting-maid," Zabina says to Zenocrate (III.iii. 177). Altogether, the Turks teach the shepherd how to conduct himself when he overcomes both Asia and Africa. Some of Tamburlaine's bloody violence thus originates with the legitimate Turk; therefore, he only imitates the civilizations that fall before him.

The dramatic case in favor of Tamburlaine is carefully constructed. When he meets the infidel Turks he is called "the scourge and wrath of God" (III.iii. 44), and the Turks are pictured as the abusers of Christians. A great point is made of the Turkish threat to the Christians, and their defeat is shown as a blessing to the West. Our sympathies are not for a moment aligned with the Turks; and, when we are forced to choose between them and Tamburlaine's Persians, we automatically ally ourselves with the Persians. The contrast is pointed up in the matching speeches of Zenocrate and Zabina: Zenocrate prays for victory, but Zabina violently asks that murdering shot rain down from heaven to dash the Scythians' brains (III.iii. 196–97). Throughout the whole scene, Tamburlaine and Zenocrate are formally pitted against Bajazeth and Zabina; and in every exchange the Turks are more violent, more bloody, and more vindictive. Finally, when they are overcome, we are explicitly informed that Tamburlaine defeats them in a fair fight, "kingly fought" (III.iii. 216). In captivity, the Turkish monarchs blasphemously curse their god; in contrast, Tamburlaine and Zenocrate turn their minds to worldly matters, for Tamburlaine calls the whole wide globe before our eyes; from India to Mexico, all the world awaits conquest.

At this point in his career, Tamburlaine does not talk of the bloody cost of conquest—he is associated in our minds with victory, not violence. The scene immediately preceding the defeat of Bajazeth contains Zenocrate's hymn of love (III.ii. 47ff) in which the empress enumerates his unwarlike attributes and answers Agydas' assertion that his nature is "vile and barbarous." Agydas' disloyalty to Tamburlaine earns him death—significantly, death by his own hand. Unable to stand before what he calls the "killing frowns" of "tyrant's rage," Agydas stabs himself in the first violent death of the play. In so doing, he earns no sympathy from the audience. Indeed, this action only makes Tamburlaine grander, for it seems to imply that Tamburlaine's very frown deprives his opponents of the will to resist. In this second movement of the play, we have seen the barbarous Tamburlaine taught violence by his defeated, civilized Turks; but we have not seen him engaged in bloody action.

The third, climactic, movement of the play begins with Act IV and the appearance of the soldan of Egypt. Our sympathies are still not divorced from Tamburlaine; as before, he is seen as the baseborn challenger of the established order. Because he is the rebel who dares to strike against authority, his enemies call him a "peasant ignorant/ Of lawful arms or martial discipline!" (IV.i. 65–66); and they say he is holding Zenocrate, the soldan's daughter, as his "concubine." We know, however, that these claims are mistaken on both counts. Tamburlaine may be of low birth but he is certainly not ignorant of arms, and Zenocrate is respected as a queen, not used to satisfy the tyrant's lust (IV.iii. 42).

From the beginning, we are prejudiced against Tamburlaine's latest challenger, for he fails to credit Tamburlaine with the magnificence that we know is his. The more the soldan disparages him, the more we give him our allegiance. Tamburlaine becomes the very embodiment of our desire to see the arrogant great pulled down, to see the baseborn rise and the wellborn fall, and to see legality replaced with adolescent dreams of self-fulfillment. Although the invincible world conqueror, Tamburlaine is represented as the underdog, scorned by strutting inferiors. Marlowe continues magisterially to manipulate our sympathies.

In the celebrated scene that follows (IV.ii.), Tamburlaine not only makes Bajazeth his footstool; he deliberately flaunts the established Boethian philosophy that all men rise but to fall. Throughout the scene, the Turks continue to express the conventional Tudor-medieval views of greatness: worldly power is transitory, but birthright is uncallengeable. In contrast, Tamburlaine, like Jehovah, uses the world for his footstool. He rules Fortune; and cries of *memento mori* do not apply to him since he rises above ordinary mortality. Now his speech is filled with blood, and war is praised independent of its rewards. Although battles earn prizes, both jewels with which to dress Zenocrate and crowns with which to deck subordinate generals, war and blood are goods in their own right:

> . . . when the sky shall wax as red as blood,
> It shall be said I made it red myself,
> To make me think of naught but blood and war.
>   (IV.ii. 53–55)

Now, in this fourth act, he earns his title "bloody Tamburlaine." But the word *blood* has an ambiguous meaning. When Cosroe is dying, he says, "My bloodless body waxeth chill and cold" (II.vii. 42); and Bajazeth locked harmless in his cage says, "My veins are pale, my sinews hard and dry," (IV.iv. 95). Blood becomes the necessary ingredient of life, the symbol of vitality; and one has life in proportion to the quantity of blood one is able to expend. "Bloody war" is thus an expression of full human vitality, and to describe Tamburlaine as *bloody* is to attribute to him quantities of vital energies without which one dries, chills, and grows cold. War is the evidence of this vitality.

By the time we come to the last long scene of the play, we recognize that the idea of *blood* and the idea of *honor*—Tamburlaine's honor, that is—are inseparably linked. Everybody in the play, friend and enemy alike, recognizes Tamburlaine's divine qualities; and we in the audience glory in it too, perhaps against our will, certainly against our judgment. His determination to victory is signaled by his treatment of Damascus. Having refused Tamburlaine's ultimatum, the governor of Damascus sends four virgins to plead that "this man, or rather god of war," mercifully spare the city (V.i. 1). They find Tamburlaine dressed in black and, according to the stage direction, "very melancholy." Although his response is filled with regret, his honor demands that Damascus and they be destroyed. Tamburlaine seems driven beyond his will to be the instrument of his own bloody genius. He grieves that he must slaughter "the turtles frayed out of their nests" (V.ii. 1), and asks the virgins, whom he is about to kill, and his audience, to pity him for the frightful deed he must commit. Only a superman, his attitude suggests, could withstand the virgins' pleas; only a man of godlike power could resist their innocence.

We do not concur in Tamburlaine's decision to stick to his resolve, but we are supposed to see the courage it requires and to be awestruck. This scene exploits the common human fascination with the repulsive—and that it is effective tells us a good deal about ourselves. It is true, we are protected from some pain in that the virgins are uncharacterized and thus do not appeal to our imagination. Their pleas are conventionally rhetorical,[11] and their executioner does not touch our passions either. With almost cavalier nonchalance, he tells Techelles to find his horsemen and "straight go charge a few of them/ To charge these dames and show my servant, Death,/ Sitting in scarlet on their armèd spears" (V.ii. 53–55). Only because Tamburlaine is above human pity is he able to possess that "honor." Only one touched by Fortune can follow such "honor, that consists in shedding blood/ When men presume to manage arms with him" (V.ii. 414–15).

We are not asked to dwell on the details of the cruelty involved in the slaughter of the virgins since the scene is completed in less than a hundred lines, and we then pass on to Tamburlaine's apostrophe to Zenocrate (V.ii. 72–127), a speech calculated to shorten any extended sensation of terror. The apostrophe has struck many readers as strained, as though Marlowe aimed in it at *"fine writing."*[12] It may be. Marlowe has a ticklish dramaturgical problem: he must control our inflamed emotions, but he must not undercut the effects of horror he has just created. To solve this difficulty, he raises the whole matter of conquest to the level of philosophical disquisition. The passage begins: "Ah, fair Zenocrate! Divine Zenocrate!/ Fair is too foul an epithet for thee . . ." (V.ii. 72–73). It continues:

> . . . neither Persians' sovereign nor the Turk
> Troubled my senses with conceit of foil
> So much by much as doth Zenocrate.
> What is beauty, saith my sufferings, then?
> If all the pens that ever poets held
> Had fed the feelings of their masters' thoughts,

. . . .
Yet should there hover in their restless heads
One thought, one grace, one wonder, at the least,
Which into words no virtue can digest. . . .
                    (V.ii. 94–99; 108–10)

The passage concludes:

. . . every warrior that is rapt with love
Of fame, of valor, and of victory
Must needs have beauty beat on his conceits.
I thus conceiving and subduing both

. . . .
Shall give the world to note, for all my birth,
That virtue solely is the sum of glory,
And fashions men with true nobility.
                    (V.ii. 117–20, 125–27)

In this ambiguous speech, Tamburlaine seems to be equating his love for Zenocrate with his restless search (love) for fame, valor, and victory. Beauty seems to be the awareness of human limitation both in love and in glory, and he alone is not paralyzed by it. He alone controls it; he, the extraordinary man, has true virtue. *Virtue* here has Italian overtones and seems to be synonymous with power. In Machiavelli's *Prince*, that textbook of Renaissance politics, *virtù* is the full development of the human intellect and will; it is ruthless determination combined with exceptional ability to conceive and carry through a plan of action. In short, Tamburlaine is here telling us that in loving Zenocrate and in overcoming all his enemies, including the innocent virgins, he demonstrates his possession of true virtue: naked power. This is but the final statement of his awareness that he is one with the gods. It is a mistake to read this speech as a revelation of a "very real conflict in the hero's mind,"[13] for the play does not ask us to inquire into Tamburlaine's psyche. If we read this speech as evidence of a division of his nature, the character becomes wildly inconsistent. Indeed, to do so makes him as complicated as Hamlet, which he patently is not. It seems much wiser to see it as the exposition (if a rather confused one) of a "philosophical ideal of virtue."[14]

Immediately following the disquisition on beauty and virtue, Bajazeth and Zabina are brought forward. The Turkish emperor is still within his bars, and in a moment, according to the stage directions (following l. 241), he "brains himself against the cage"; when his queen discovers him, she goes mad and "runs against the cage and brains herself." The scene has its ludicrous aspects, and no doubt certain hardy Elizabethans laughed uproariously. The act has kept us at a high pitch of terror to which Bajazeth's concluding words have contributed:

> Ah, fair Zabina, we may curse his power,
> The heavens may frown, the earth for anger quake,
> But such a star hath influence in his sword
> As rules the skies and countermands the gods
> More than Cimmerian Styx or Destiny.
> (V.ii. 167–71)

The laughter that this scene occasions is derisive and ugly, but it is directed against the bragging Bajazeth. In the end, Tamburlaine has not only conquered the Turk's armies, he has overcome the Turk's spirit. The monarch, who once could only agree with flatterers that "all flesh quakes at [my] magnificence" (III.i. 48), now sees that he must end his dreadful ecstasies. Zabina, recognizing the godlike power of Tamburlaine, protests that there is no Mahomet to end their monstrous slaveries. The longer they lament their fate, the more invincible Tamburlaine seems. The world is too small to include both Tamburlaine and another king. Lesser men, like Theridamas, may follow or die, like Cosroe, but they can have no independent existence. Tamburlaine is not an ordinary general, he is a natural, cataclysmic, phenomenon. Marlowe asks us to see the world through his eyes, to identify our interests with his.

The final scene of *Part One* is a last weighing and considering of Tamburlaine's attributes. His cruelty is now underscored, for Zenocrate says:

> But see, another bloody spectacle!
> Ah, wretched eyes, the enemies of my heart,
> How are ye glutted with these grievous objects,
> And tell my soul more tales of bleeding ruth!
> (V.ii. 276–79)

Eugene M. Waith has remarked that Zenocrate both "presents the conventional view of hubris more convincingly than any other character, and shows the inadequacy of this view in judging Tamburlaine."[15] Certainly his godlike power, his irresistible drive to domination, gets full treatment in this last scene; and his strength is underscored by the death, presumably by exhaustion, of the king of Arabia. Then Tamburlaine, this godlike figure, condescends to give the soldan a reprieve from his death sentence because he is father of Zenocrate. In a "god-like caprice,"[16] Tamburlaine allows him to escape the fury of his sword:

> The god of war resigns his room to me,
> Meaning to make me general of the world.
> Jove, viewing me in arms, looks pale and wan,
> Fearing my power should pull him from his throne.
> Where'er I come the Fatal Sisters sweat,
> And grisly Death, by running to and fro
> To do their ceaseless homage to my sword.
>
> (V.ii. 387–93)

Then follows a passage (V.ii. 394–415) filled with "apocalyptic imagery" reminiscent of that in the biblical Book of Revelation. Some careful readers have thought "it is very difficult not to see in Tamburlaine's speech, so incongruous in its setting and received with such astonishing calm by his hearers, Marlowe's ironic mockery of the prophetic vision of the God of Judgment."[17] Tamburlaine has ascended the very throne of heaven.

And this is the tone with which *Tamburlaine, Part One* ends. We can detect no hint that the bloody conqueror cannot expect continued success, that any power divine or human can restrain him. In a final tableau, he and his queen, surrounded by their subordinate kings and generals, sit crowned, high above all others; as F. P. Wilson says, they are "a happy warrior and a happy lover" (p. 19). The conquest of the world is complete. Cruelty and force of arms have demonstrated their superiority to cleverness, ordinary loyalties, birth, legality, even love itself. All bows before power, even our respect. We are awestruck at the spectacle, horrified to find our baser ambitions released, or even fulfilled, in this bloody Tamburlaine. By careful arrangement of action, Marlowe has guided our sympathies against our judgments. The rhetoric and structure of the play combine to support its outrageous theme.

III   Tamburlaine, *Part Two*

Though the parts of *Tamburlaine* were originally published together as a unit "Divided into two Tragical Discourses," they were conceived separately. With *Part Two* Marlowe attempted to capitalize on the success he had achieved with what is now known as *Tamburlaine, Part One.* Structurally *Part Two* repeats the simple pattern of action used in *Part One,* for both plays are straightforward dramatic crescendos, each incident being more bloody and more violent than the one preceding it. In both plays each movement is larger and bolder than what had gone before. *Part One* had ended at a pitch of such excitement that *Part Two* runs the risk of seeming anti-climactic; but that it is not is a measure of Marlowe's accomplishment.

Tamburlaine, Part Two, like *Part One,* may be divided into three main movements. In both plays, a first climax is reached at the end of Act II; a second, midway in the play; and the last, near the end. Dramaturgically, *Part Two* is like *Part One*; thematically, *Part Two* is original. Marlowe avoids threatening monotony by introducing new ideas—he pours some new wine into an old bottle, as it were. Harry Levin has proposed provocatively that "the first [play] treats of love and war, the second of war and death."[18] It may be more accurate to say, however, that in *Part One* Tamburlaine is concerned with worldly conquest and in *Part Two* with spiritual conquest, ultimately in his conquest of himself.

Being mortal, though a demi-god, Tamburlaine is subject to certain human exigencies. The questions which he faces in *Part Two* are these: how can he accept mortal separation from Zenocrate, the weaknesses of his successors, and at last his own death, and yet retain his claims to superhuman power? None of the trials to which his flesh is heir overcomes him; throughout *Part Two* he goes from spiritual triumph to spiritual triumph, even as he went from military victory to military victory in *Part One.* The tone of the second play is less insouciant than the first, but the quality of the verse is generally sustained. It is to be expected that the general atmosphere should be less youthful, for the theme of *Part Two* is essentially grave. Tamburlaine—and Marlowe—face harder problems in the much less fairy-tale world of *Part Two*. The new play shows an appreciable growth.

The kinds of opponents Tamburlaine meets in *Part Two* are also markedly different from those in *Part One*. In the first play he had no serious opposition; Mycetes, Cosroe, even Bajazeth, were little more than toy soldiers awaiting toppling. In the second play Tamburlaine's enemies are not only more vigorous, they are cleverer and—of primary importance in drama—more interesting. The play begins with Orcanes, who is worthy of our genuine respect and who makes a considerable contrast to his counterpart, Mycetes, whom we met in Act I of *Part One*. Once again, Tamburlaine is not brought on stage until we have met two subordinate kings—these were Mycetes and Cosroe in *Part One*; they are Orcanes and Sigismund in *Part Two*. Structurally and technically, Marlowe imitates himself.

In *Part Two* Orcanes and Sigismund, the Christian king of Hungary, make a pact against Tamburlaine, their common enemy. Their power is made vivid for us by a careful, rhetorical listing of their allies: Sigismund and the Hungarians are joined by the "Slavonians, Almains, Rutters, Muffs, and Danes" (I.i.22; 58), as well as by Orcanes and thirteen additional nations (I.i. 61–64). This exotic roll-call is a rhetorical device for expanding the imaginative horizon which Marlowe has used before.

Tamburlaine's stature is enlarged by the worthiness of his opponents, but his entrance is delayed to increase the theatrical suspense. Before he appears, we meet Callapine and Almeda, Callapine's jailor and Tamburlaine's hireling. Callapine is the son of Bajazeth—he was not spoken of in *Part One*—but he is less a braggart than his father was, and he is shrewder. He bribes Almeda, his jailor, to release him from Tamburlaine's bondage by promising him Tamburlaine-like rewards. Almeda is so unlike the monarch to whose wealth he aspires that we can only laugh; as a result, the whole exchange defines Tamburlaine's vaulting spirit.

Our first meeting with Tamburlaine in *Part Two*, like our initial meeting with him in *Part One*, brings him accompanied by persons ordinarily associated with gentleness. In *Part One* he appeared with the beautiful captive princess, Zenocrate; in *Part*

Two he appears with his queen and their three young sons. In both theatrically conceived scenes we see Tamburlaine's seriousness of purpose and his concern for martial affairs. The scene in *Part Two* asserts the primacy of the irascible powers over the amorous ones, as Waith observes (p. 79); and when Tamburlaine storms grandiloquently at his weak son but promises great rewards to his warlike younger sons, he dramatizes this nature. The sons who are willing to "swim through pools of blood/ Or make a bridge of murdered carcasses" (I.iv. 92–93) are his "lovely boys."

Tamburlaine's magnitude is also dramatized by the appearance of Theridamas and his entourage, followed a moment later by Techelles, Usumcasane, and their trains. The stage is filled with banners and drums in a pageant of invincible power and the "scourge of God" is addressed as "our earthly god/ Whose looks make this inferior world to quake" (I.vi. 11–12). The rhetorical and ritualistic conclusion of the scene raises the whole action out of our ordinary human experience; we are back in the world of demi-gods ruled over by Tamburlaine, a world of assertion and magnificence far above "policy," alliances, and calculation. This world of simple, mad self-assertion is uncomplicated by thought—that is, by qualification—and by compromise. Such a world is possible in the theater by combining words, movement, and action, as Marlowe does here. Tamburlaine is demonstrably stronger than all the military forces of the world combined, and the playgoer knows it from the banners and eloquence. However, as we have noted, spiritual, not military, matters will be dominant in this play.

Act I repeats the view of Tamburlaine that we had from *Part One*. Act I, *Part One*, showed us Tamburlaine boasting of his power over Fortune and the world; Act I, *Part Two*, shows us Tamburlaine, "our earthly god," shaming the sun with his might. The first acts of the two plays are dramaturgically parallel, and effective. Marlowe, as always, writes for stage action, making full use of sounds, sights, and devices; and so must his play be read.

We are quickly shown in Act II that the world of politics is more corrupt than Tamburlaine's world of power. Sigismund, the Christian king of Hungary, who only a moment before was

seen swearing to live in peace with Orcanes—"By Him that made
the world and saved my soul" (I.ii. 56)—now breaks his word,
arguing jesuitically that Christian oaths do not hold with infidels.
His kind of duplicity is foreign to Tamburlaine, and we recoil
to him from Sigismund's Christian hypocrisy. Here Marlowe may
or may not have expressed his private conviction concerning
Christianity—much ink has been spilled over the matter. The
fact is that Sigismund's conduct frees the audience from its natural allegiance to its own, Christian, kind. As Steane says, "When
Sigismund betrays his ally, Christianity loses face and Christians
forfeit the right to be morally smug about Tamburlaine" (p. 66).

If we have not been estranged from Sigismund by his faithlessness, the next scene, in which Orcanes discovers that he has
been betrayed, persuades us to oppose Sigismund. Orcanes'
splendid speech begins:

> Can there be such deceit in Christians
> Or treason in the fleshly heart of man,
> Whose shape is figure of the highest God?
> (II.ii. 36–38)

This speech continues with what has been called "the best clue
to Marlowe's religious thought,"[19] but what his thought actually
was is impossible to determine. What we know is that Orcanes'
speech is dramatically appropriate, for we see that this Turk is
a better Christian than the Christian. When Sigismund is defeated by Orcanes, he attributes his fall to "my accursed and
hateful perjury" (II.iii. 3). There is a significant difference between this defeat in *Part Two* and the comparable defeats in
Part One. In *Part One*, the philosophical speculations—"Nature,
that framed us of four elements" and so on (II.vii. 18ff)—vindi-
cated conquest and worldly success. These scenes in *Part Two*,
in contrast, lead us to wonder if the universe is just after all.
Both plays are philosophical in that they both excite us to thought
about ultimate values. *Part One* glorifies worldly conquest, but
Part Two posits the conventional views against such glorification
and, as we shall see, shouts them down.

Marlowe's dramatic problem is now intensified. Orcanes has
been shown to be so noble in adversity and so thoughtful in
defeat that he threatens to gain some of the homage we once

paid Tamburlaine. In showing the faithlessness of the Christians and the honor of the Turks, Marlowe is in danger of giving to the Turks some of the fascinated sympathy we have reserved for Tamburlaine. More important, he is in danger of implying that Tamburlaine is an aberration rather than a fulfillment of natural law. If Sigismund can expect defeat for violating the Christian codes, can we not expect Tamburlaine likewise to fall from his all conquering majesty? The question is hardly raised before it is answered.

By theatrical maneuver and emphasis, Marlowe directs our attention from Sigismund and Orcanes back to Tamburlaine, and we see him in a new, extravagant situation where he triumphs, contrary to all logic and common sense. When Zenocrate, his queen, dies (II.iv.), her death might be expected to remind him that he is less than Jove, for her death is a direct challenge to his omnipotence. Miss Mahood has proposed that the scene "marks the beginning of the conqueror's disillusion" (p. 60), but this statement does not seem to be right; it is too simple, too doctrinaire; and it also neglects the pervasive histrionic nature of the play. Marlowe is not debating the nature of power with us; he overwhelms us with all the theatrical resources at his disposal.

Act II, scene iv, Zenocrate's death, begins with a formal lament on the passing of the queen to heavenly entertainment,[20] and it continues with an eloquent lyric:

> . . . had she lived before the siege of Troy,
> Helen, whose beauty summoned Greece to arms
> And drew a thousand ships to Tenedos,
> Had not been named in Homer's Iliads;
> Her name had been in every line he wrote.
> (II.iv.86–90)

What interests us now—and indeed throughout the scene, for Zenocrate has never been sharply enough outlined to hold our attention in her own right—is how Tamburlaine reacts to the death of the one he loves. When he himself comes to die, he tells his son Amyras: "Let not thy love exceed thine honor, son,/ Nor bar [from] thy mind that magnanimity/ That nobly must admit necessity" (V.iii. 199–201). And *honor* for Tamburlaine is the bloody assertion of self over all physical obstacles. In spiritual matters this means, in a kind of perversion of Stoic doctrine, that he must not yield to death, love, or any weakness about him; rather, *honor* requires that he assert himself before "necessity."

But, when Zenocrate is dead, his audacity before inescapable adversity is overpowering. Always extravagant in gesture, he is inordinately immoderate now. He orders the earth wounded with Techelles' sword, the frame of heaven broken by cannon, the city of her death burned, and her body, wrapped in sheets of gold, added to his entourage. Logically, this reaction is preposterous; but Tamburlaine is beyond logic. The scene is calculated to so blind us with spectacle that we cannot think—fireworks simulate the burning of a city, explosives suggest the firing of cannons, and pageantry ennobles the body of Zenocrate. These stage effects have been used before, but never in such conjunction. The meditations of Orcanes are forgotten in a blaze of fire, explosive, and Marlovian rhetoric. All the careful objections to Tamburlaine are left far behind in this display of power. Nothing we have yet seen in either play of *Tamburlaine* can touch this spectacle.

The first movement of *Tamburlaine, Part One* ended with the conclusion of Act II; surrounded by tributary monarchs, Tamburlaine crowned himself king of Persia. The first movement of *Part Two* ends with similar grandeur: Tamburlaine defies death itself. The second movement of *Part One* dealt with Tamburlaine's triumph over his military adversary, Bajazeth; the second movement of *Part Two* deals, as we shall see, with his triumph over a new spiritual obstacle: his son's cowardice. With theatrical effectiveness, Marlowe has Tamburlaine subordinate his paternal affections to the glory of war, and *Part Two* moves to its second climax.

In the first scene of the second movement (III.i.), all of the kings opposing Tamburlaine parade across the stage. As they raise anew the arguments against him, we are reminded of his base birth and his usurpation of authority; and we are told once more that Fortune has long followed "the martial sword of mighty Tamburlaine" (III.i. 28). Orcanes and Callapine have by now united their forces, confident that Fortune will return to her ordinary inconstancy. This scene not only reiterates the conventional charges against the conqueror; it gives us a brief laugh as well. When Callapine assures Almeda, the ambitious jailor, that he will get the crown for which he yearns, the dramatic tension of warlike spectacle is momentarily relieved, and we are grateful for a moment of respite. When the enemy pageant has passed into the wings, Tamburlaine's spectacle appears. We see the burning town and the gilden hearse of Zenocrate borne on the shoulders of martial kings; we hear drums and formal speeches; but none of this action displays any private emotion. Tamburlaine is beyond personality; indeed, his great speech in this scene deals with the art of war, not love—almost as though he wanted to reestablish the relative worth of things (III.ii. 53–92). Impervious to grief, he displays an almost godlike knowledge of warfare; and, instructing his sons, he sounds like Jove.

But the scene does not remain formal, and shortly it becomes theatrical in a new way. Calyphas, the eldest of his sons, indicates a weakhearted interest in his father's martial instructions: "My lord, but this is dangerous to be done;/ We may be slain or wounded ere we learn" (III.ii. 93–94). And with this statement Marlowe has brought us to the second of Tamburlaine's spiritual trials, the first being Zenocrate's death. To show his contempt for the wounds that the son fears, Tamburlaine lances his own flesh and allows his blood to stream from his arm. "Blood is the god of war's rich livery," he says (III.ii. 116). In a masochistic baptismal ceremony, he invites his sons to wash their hands in his blood. There has been blood aplenty in these plays, but never before has Tamburlaine himself been the executioner, nor has he before been wounded. With his blood flowing as if from a fountain of virility, it is difficult to imagine a more vivid example of bravura, perverse though it may be. Tamburlaine demonstrates his superiority to ordinary human necessity before our eyes. Neither the death of his queen nor the weakness of his son can dampen his ardor or limit his conquest. He remains above ordinary considerations.

Tamburlaine's relationship to his sons holds our primary attention through this movement of the play. As early as the first act of *Part One* Tamburlaine acknowledged his mortality (I.ii. 231–37), his awareness here of his own approaching death sharpens his insistence that his sons continue his purposes. His relationship to his sons is explicitly contrasted to two other parent-son relationships in the play. The first of these is Callapine's duty to the memory of his father, Bajazeth; and, since his defense of his father's reputation is his chief end in life, his piety makes Calyphas' weakness seem the more reprehensible. Amyras and Celebrinus, Tamburlaine's other sons, are determined, like Callapine, to guard their father's great name. The second contrast in the play of the parent-child situation results when Olympia's husband is slain by one of Tamburlaine's bullets (III.iv.). Olympia kills her own son because she cannot allow him to fall into the enemy's hands. As she casts the bodies of both her husband and her son into funeral flames and prepares her own suicide, Theridamas surprises her and frustrates her action (III.iv. 34); and because her warlike valor recommends her to him, he lays siege to her heart but is unsuccessful. Tamburlaine and Olympia are two of a kind and both are larger than lifesize; indeed, Olympia's murder of her son foreshadows Tamburlaine's killing of his. Her spartan slaughter prepares us to accept Tamburlaine's.

Introduced by these scenes with Olympia, Tamburlaine's relationship to his sons now reaches its climax. As in *Part One,* Tamburlaine challenges his enemies, threatening them with violent dishonor if they persist in opposing him. Calyphas, unlike his younger brothers, does not participate in the battle that follows, but remains in his tent, playing cards. When the battle is ended, Tamburlaine drags the recalcitrant Calyphas from his shelter and, resisting the pleas of his generals and his other sons, delivers "martial justice on [Calyphas'] wretched soul" (IV.ii. 21). He prepares to slay him:

> Here, Jove, receive his fainting soul
> A form not meet to give that subject essence
> Whose matter is the flesh of Tamburlaine,
> Wherein an incorporeal spirit moves,
> Made of the mould whereof thyself consists. . . .
> (IV.ii. 36–40)

Shouting defiance of the ruling gods who sent him such a false son, he stabs his son to death before our eyes:

> By Mahomet, thy mighty friend, I swear,
> In sending to my issue such a soul,

> Created of the massy dregs of earth,
> The scum and tartar of the elements,
> Wherein was neither courage, strength, or wit,
> But folly, sloth, and damnèd idleness,
> Thou has procured a greater enemy
> Than he that darted mountains at thy head. . .
>   (IV.ii. 46–53)

Tamburlaine conceives of himself as a spirit opposed to the "massy dregs of earth" and explicitly challenges Jove himself. The scene induces a shudder of horror, both in us and in the characters on stage; but the slaying is not simply barbarous, despite the terms from which the conqueror operates, for it contains a kind of wild justice. Calyphas is flesh of his flesh; and his spirit, we are told, must be of his spirit. When it is not, Tamburlaine amputates it, even as he wounds his own arm in pursuing the honor that his nature requires. It is his duty to cleanse the earth of the "scum and tartar of the elements. . ." (IV.ii. 49), and he must, he says, "scourge the pride of such as heaven abhors" (IV.ii. 74)—even if it be his own son. Far from being a defeat, the murder of Calyphas marks, therefore, the triumph of this violent spirit. The worst that the mortal world can bring does not daunt him—not the death of Zenocrate, the infidelity of the faithful like Almeda, or the weakness of his son. He is stalwart before them all; and, if he be mad, there is divinity in his madness.

Tamburlaine's greatest trial, his own death, remains; but this too fails to conquer him. The play's final ambiguous movement begins with Act IV, scene iv. It is emblematic—the other scenes have for the most part not been—and deserves a nearly allegorical reading. The scene opens with Tamburlaine driving a chariot pulled by his captive kings; and, though the spectacle may strike us as excessive, it originally "appears to have given the play an important measure of its popularity."[21] Once more Tamburlaine asserts that he is "the scourge of highest Jove" (IV.iv. 23), and we are supposed to see that the earth's mighties are ruled by his primordial energy. Furthermore, we learn that when "Jove, esteeming me too good for earth" finally raises him "Above the threefold astracism of heaven" (IV.iv. 60, 62), his sons will continue to reduce the vanity of kings. The Tamburlaine scourge will not end with his death, for his sons will carry on in his spirit. The next scene (V.i.) deals with Babylon, symbolically the very seat of self-indulgence and luxury; and it summarizes the conqueror's duty and accomplishment. The governor of Babylon, refusing to accept the advice and the prayers of his citizens, resists Tamburlaine's attack, for his vanity exceeds his judgment. Tamburlaine, easily conquering the city, condemns its inhabitants to be drowned:

> . . . I myself
> The wrathful messenger of mighty Jove,
> That with his sword hath quailed all earthly kings
> Could not persuade you to submission. . .
> (V.i. 91–94)

As a consequence the governor is hanged in chains for soldiers to shoot at. Babylon had earned its mighty punishment; and by extension, so have all the other kings who have stood out against him. Though cruel, Tamburlaine has cleansed the world of vanity. He fulfills his destiny. In Act V, *Part One,* Tamburlaine condemned the innocent virgins to violent death for resisting him. Here, in Act V, *Part Two,* he condemns the citizens of Babylon to drowning. The pattern of action remains parallel to the end.

And now at last Tamburlaine seems to be overcome, but his seeming fall is, probably, deceptive. His spirit remains unconquered to the end. When Babylon is overcome, Tamburlaine orders "the Turkish Alcoran/ And all the heaps of superstitious books" to be burnt (V.i. 171–72). He brags of the priests, kinsmen, and friends of Mahomet whom he has slain "And yet I live untouched by Mahomet" (V.i. 180); "Mahomet remains in hell" (V.ii. 195) and does not come to wreak vengeance. Or so it seems at first. And then—"But stay," Tamburlaine says, "I feel myself distempered suddenly" (V.i. 216). The sudden illness follows too close upon the defiance of Mahomet to be dramatically unrelated. Apparently, his last defiance is challenged by heaven.

But it is not challenged very much, for even illness cannot falter Tamburlaine: "But, forth, ye vassals! Whatsoe'er it be,/ Sickness or death can never conquer me" (V.i. 219–20). And, in point of fact, sickness and death do not "conquer" him—if one

[65]

takes "conquer" to mean that his spirit is vanquished. From the beginning, he has known that death awaited him; he differed from lesser men in possessing an unyielding soul, not a deathless body. Unlike the Christian Sigismund, who recognized his perjury, confessed it, and received his punishment, the pagan Tamburlaine acknowledges no error. He remains defiant:

> What daring god torments my body thus
> And seeks to conquer mighty Tamburlaine?
> Shall sickness prove me now to be a man,
> That have been termed the terror of the world?
>   (V.iii. 42–45)

He can be whipped with pain, but, even in his dying moments, he conquers threatening multitudes merely by showing himself. In his final agonies, he sees death as but one more field to conquer:

> But I perceive my martial strength is spent.
> In vain I strive and rail against those powers
> That mean t'invest me in a higher throne,
> As much too high for this disdainful earth.
>   (V.iii. 119–22)

In this concluding scene Tamburlaine transcends human suffering. Not untouched, he is able to rise above it; our response "is neither sympathy nor pity, but predominantly awe."[22] There is no slight hint in this final scene that Tamburlaine (or we) can think his career anything but "right." Tamburlaine has lived according to the requirements of his nature, and this play is a paean of praise to his indomitable spirit.

Tamburlaine does not leave the world without providing for a successor. The spirit of conquest, the unbridled cruelty which was central to his accomplishments, will be continued in his remaining sons; and he has prepared them for their responsibilities. The play ends on a note of magnificent praise:

> For earth hath spent the pride of all her fruit,
> Meet heaven and earth, and here let all things end,
> And heaven consumed his choicest living fire.
> Let earth and heaven his timeless death deplore,
> For both their worths will equal him no more.
>   (V.iii. 249–53)

Caesarism: *Tamburlaine the Great*

Though "Tamburlaine, the scourge of God, must die" (V.iii. 248)—the line is extraordinarily memorable and even ambiguous —his death is triumphant.

Tamburlaine, Part Two is not so fine a play as *Part One*, as almost all critics have agreed. It lacks the youthful, even adolescent, gaiety of the earlier play; and it sometimes lacks verbal freshness. The eloquence sometimes strikes us as shouting. In Act III, where Marlowe allows Sigismund to become too persuasive, he even miscalculates and sacrifices some of the admiration we are supposed to feel for Tamburlaine. The scenes between Theridamas and Olympia are too stiff, too cold, and the scene in which Tamburlaine is drawn in his chariot by the captive kings (IV.iv) is filled with rant. The language of this play has been frequently commented upon, but what has not been so frequently noted is that in *Part Two* Marlowe relies on theatrical display as much as he does on verbal rhetoric. Suicides, murders, burning cities, captive monarchs, flowing blood, and parades of kings supplement, when they do not replace, the verbal fireworks of *Part One*. *Tamburlaine, Part Two* is more obviously a theatrical exercise than *Part One* and must always be examined as such. Organized on the simple linear pattern of *Part One*, it depends very heavily on stage effects for its success.

Tamburlaine, Part Two is a scenario for the theater, as all of Marlowe's plays are, for Marlowe is as always a brilliant technician. But this play also exhibits Marlowe's habitual concerns and convictions: he asks us here to admire power as a greater value than justice, or mercy, or charity. This play, like *Dido, Queen of Carthage, Doctor Faustus*, and *Edward II*, raises questions of the nature and limits of authority. Surely we are intended to feel, as the play ends, that the courageous man who is true to his nature, no matter how violent, and who is persistent in his aspirations, no matter how lawless, deserves special respect. Even the gods cannot take from him the honor won by his determination.

When we have put the play aside, we must be repulsed by the cruelty we have been asked to admire; and we must grieve that we can take delight in observing the infliction of needless pain. We may even laugh at the ludicrousness of some of Tamburlaine's ranting; but, sunk in the plays, we are fascinated out of thought. In one sense, these plays are immoral; for they persuade us to applaud what is despicable. Marlowe has constructed two plays glorifying one aspect of the irrational revolutionary spirit which has become characteristic of succeeding Romantic centuries—the love of unrestrained power. We may not like what he shows us—the nature of that unrestrained power—but, as serious students of drama and history, we cannot pretend that these temptations do not exist; nor, remembering naziism and other absolute doctrines of our time, can we pretend that they do not matter.

CHAPTER 4

The Drama of Doctor Faustus

I *The* Faustus *Problems*

THE TRAGICAL HISTORY of the Life and Death of Doctor Faustus was, like *Tamburlaine*, popular in its own time, and it not only held public attention for generations but even inspired folklore. Gossip said that, on one occasion, the actor playing Faustus conjured up a real devil. This broke up the performance, as well it might, and the players spent the night "in reading and in prayer."[1] The play is still regularly staged; for like the Elizabethans, modern men see something archetypal in Marlowe's aspiring doctor. He seems "born under one law, to another bound." He lives in divided and distinguished worlds where fact and faith conflict; he exists where there is a radical distinction between the eternal and the temporal, between the sacred and the profane. Perhaps because he defines an aspect of our own experience, Marlowe's play is much studied.

And yet the date, the text, and the meaning of *Doctor Faustus* offer scholarly difficulties of the first magnitude. We do not know whether the play was an early work written shortly after Marlowe's success with *Tamburlaine* or a product of his last years. A ballad dealing with Faustus "the great Cungerer" and Greene's *Friar Bacon and Friar Bungay* which alludes to the

Marlowe play both appeared about 1589. In style *Faustus* is similar to *Tamburlaine* (1587). In both we hear the "mighty line" which was to be echoed and parodied for decades. Both plays center on a single heroic figure and follow his progress to his death. Both are essentially historical and episodic as compared to the dynamic and complex *Edward II*, Marlowe's late play. Both have close structural affinities to the morality drama, affinities which the later plays do not obviously possess. David Bevington has recently shown how the low comedy of *Doctor Faustus* is like the comedy of the anachronistic morality plays. The comic is "an integral expression of the Psychomachia," he says.[2] From this evidence, we, with E. K. Chambers, would date *Doctor Faustus* as about 1588.[3]

On the other hand, the source from which Marlowe took his material, the English *History of Dr. Johann Faustus*, a translation of the German *Faustbuch* (1587), cannot be certainly dated before May, 1592. That translation survives only in what appears to be a second edition; the date of a lost first edition is unknown. The record of first production of *Faustus* is set down in Henslowe's *Diary*, as October 2, 1594; but this is unlikely to have been the play's first staging. Moreover, some critics think that the profundity of the play is that of full maturity, not that of a novice. W. W. Greg dates it in the winter of 1592-3.[4] If we are to accept the play as the culmination of Marlowe's dramatic career, we must then assume that he returned late to a style and dramatic technique that throughout his brief life he had steadily grown away from. And we must also assume that young men, newly from the university, cannot be wise. It is most likely that the play is early, written just after *Tamburlaine* in 1588 or 1589.

The date of *Doctor Faustus* is only the first of the play's perplexing problems, for the text is another. The play was first published in a short, corrupt edition, nearly a dozen years after Marlowe's death (1604), and it was issued in a larger and different form a dozen years after that (1616). The first edition runs to 1,485 lines, the second to 2,131, the standard length. Scholars are not sure which part of either was written by Marlowe. Some refuse him all the comic scenes; others, only the major portions of them. Nearly all deny him the authorship of the complete play as it appeared in 1616. Although it is generally assumed that the play was planned by Marlowe,[5] it is also thought that certain scenes, not interesting him greatly, were farmed out to Thomas Dekker or Samuel Rowley or Thomas Nashe or to another of the London hacks. In 1602 Henslowe paid William Bird and Samuel Rowley four pounds for "adicyones in doctor fostes." None of Marlowe's contemporaries is likely to have leaped at the job of collaboration during his lifetime, for he was notoriously quarrelsome.

Indeed, it appears that the principal evidence for denying the full text to Marlowe is, finally, subjective. When we assume two hands, we trust "the genuine stylistic impression of an honest and capable critic."[6] Presumably analyses of style and dramaturgy can be passed over as mechanical. Professor George Coffin Taylor, for example, has noted Marlowe's peculiar predilection for *now* at the beginning of sentences, a predilection personal enough to distinguish his from another's style. He finds that the so-called additions to *Faustus* "run about as high in *now's* as the portions" of the play regularly assigned to Marlowe.[7] It seems likely to many that Marlowe, like Homer, Dante, and Shakespeare, sometimes nodded; more, that he sometimes dropped off into esthetic slumber altogether. The burden of proof rests with those who deny the general integrity of the texts, and the evidence they offer must surely be sturdier than "taste."

The question whether every scene of *The Tragical History* was written unaided by Christopher Marlowe may well be academic. We must regard the play as having some integrity or it becomes a heap of jewels dazzling in their disorder; and it is demonstrably more than that. No English drama with the possible exception of *Everyman* strikes us with the unique force of *Doctor Faustus*. In this respect, it is rather like Sophocles' *Oedipus Tyrannos*: it has an overwhelming single effect. It is true, not all the episodes in it are as poetical as we might like them to be; but, before we condemn the play for that, we must acknowledge that poetry is only one kind of theatrical expression; a play is more than its speeches. Professor Clemen talks of Marlowe's willingness to "pander to the audience's fondness for spectacle,"[8] but we have difficulty understanding why costuming in the theater is shameful or striking staging contemptible.

The issue to raise about *Doctor Faustus* is, therefore, not that spectacle is used, but the end to which it is put. Marlowe's gorgeous shows, like Inigo Jones's, like Jonson's, are high art when they illuminate the human spirit. Artistic merit depends on the quality of the conception and the clarity of the expression, not on the nature of the machinery. Marlowe did not call on his verbal muse when he designed the middle sections of *Faustus*, but recent productions have demonstrated what many have suspected: they are theatrically effective.[9] If we study the relationship of the parts, we may end with greater pleasure from the total play. We may even come to a fuller comprehension of what Marlowe was trying to accomplish and, as a result, have greater respect for his dramaturgical accomplishments.

II *The First Part of* Faustus

Goethe, whose greatest work deals with Faustus, marveled at the beautiful organization of Marlowe's play. "How greatly it is all planned!" he said.[10] Although the play is divided into five acts of more or less equal length and although all the acts except the second are introduced by a chorus summarizing the approaching action, the original texts and many modern reprints do not indicate these helpful subdivisions. Marlowe clearly had the Classical five-act structure in mind when composing, and the relationships of scenes and acts may be profitably studied.[11] To point up the structural and thematic development of the play, each act can be given a subtitle. Act I could be called "The Decision"; Act II, "The Contract"; Act III, "The Challenge to Religious Power"; Act IV, "The Disintegration of Power"; and Act V might be called "The Reckoning." Within each act Marlowe's dramatic method is simple; in the very broadest terms, it is essentially statement and variation, and the variations are heightened by dramatic contrast. To avoid monotony in what is essentially a monodrama, Marlowe uses every theatrical trick from eloquence to claptrap. It behooves us to observe the dramaturgy.

The quality of the verse in Act I and Act II differs sharply from the quality of the verse in *Tamburlaine*. In *Tamburlaine* Marlowe often wrote speeches which were designed to go unexamined. The lines were to enchant, not instruct. As in the following excerpt, he used exotic names and repetitions to hypnotize us out of thought:

> MENAPHON: Your majesty shall shortly have your wish,
> And ride in triumph through Persepolis.
> TAMBURLAINE: And ride in triumph through Persepolis!
> Is it not brave to be a king, Techelles?
> Usumcasane and Theridamas,
> Is it not passing brave to be a king,
> And ride in triumph through Persepolis?
> (1. II. v. 48–54)

When Tamburlaine made love to Zenocrate, he talked neither of her nor of his love; he orated of the world he intended to possess (1. I. ii. 82ff). Characteristically his nouns and adjectives generalized experience; they did not specify it:

> My sword hath sent millions of Turks to hell,
> Slew all his priests, his kinsmen, and his friends,
> And yet I live untouched by Mahomet.
> There is a God, full of revenging wrath,
> For whom the thunder and the lightning breaks,
> Whose scourge I am, and Him will I obey.
> (2. V.i. 178–83)

The language in *Tamburlaine*, as the example indicates, creates huge cloudiness and avoids specificity; but the language of *Doctor Faustus* is different. As eloquent as that in *Tamburlaine*, it remains strongly accentual, with the lines rising often in interrogation. But the diction is not vague; the words have precise, though often abstract, meaning. In place of Jove's indefinite "revenging wrath," we now have "the fact of God." Even the geographic references are exact. In his speech, "Had I as many souls as there be stars" (I.iii. 102ff), Faustus expresses the aspiration to power so characteristic of other Marlowe heroes, but in place of vague Natolia and remote Lantchidol, Faustus plans to ". . . bind the Afric shore,/ And make that country continent to Spain . . ." (I.iii. 107–108). This definable, known world is expressed in concrete language. The two plays are unmistakably from the same pen, but in *Faustus* explicitness of diction and imagery replaces generality. This precise use of words is appropriate to the cerebral subject of *Doctor Faustus,* just as the passionate generality is appropriate to *Tamburlaine.*

Doctor Faustus begins like Marlowe's other plays with a chorus that defines the play's controlling idea. We are told that Faustus is "swoll'n with cunning of a self-conceit" (20), and the words are reinforced by exact though implied stage movement. Faustus is revealed as he "in his study sits" (28); it is night, and he is alone, surrounded by books which he picks up, opens, and puts aside. As everywhere in this play, the eye sees what the ear hears. In this scene and subsequently, we are not asked to be concerned with Faustus' humanity. Poirier correctly calls his personality "indistinct."[12] Faustus occupies a schematic world, without family or any except professional friends; and he becomes something of a symbol. His words, appearance, and action raise philosophical ideas, not queries about his private psychology. From the start he shadows forth an intellectual puzzle, and we are moved by his sufferings less because he is a man than because his temptations are recognizably our own.

In his introductory soliloquy, Faustus takes an inventory of the rational intellect and briefly dismisses each conventional category of learning. By the end of the first sixty-five lines of the play Faustus has made the choice on which all the subsequent action hangs, and the remainder of the play dramatizes the consequences of this choice: he sells his soul for limitless power. Faustus' first speech has a remarkable candor. No sentimentalist, Faustus plays for high stakes—he knows the nature of his decision, and he knows that he can expect eternal damnation if the traditional views are sound. Like Satan, he takes evil for his good and, like Macbeth, he becomes a witch. Indeed, when Faustus gets to Rome, he is cursed with bell, book, and candle, which was the traditional treatment of witches (III.ii.).

From the beginning Faustus sets himself up as a god qualified to judge merit absolutely. "A sound magician is a demi-god," he says (I.i. 63). He is the ultimate humanist, for he evaluates actions only as they affect him now. "Divinity, adieu!" he says (I.i. 49). Scarcely has he cast his lot with Satan than the Good Angel and the Bad Angel appear to him. These morality figures are easy to oversimplify. On one level they seem to represent the conflict in Faustus' mind and are thus an allegory of his psyche. But, more important, they represent eternal principles outside Faustus; through them, we come to know that Good and Bad exist in creation independent of any one man; indeed, we recognize that Good and Bad are parts of nature itself. When in the next act Faustus finally signs his contract with Mephistophilis in his own blood, he observes "My blood congeals, and I can write no more" (II.i. 61); and the clear implication in both scenes is that nature itself reacts to Faustus' actions: that the external universe is not disinterested. Instead, nature knowingly participates in the life of man and is an agency of God himself.

Dramatically, the Good and Bad Angels have another function. They reappear on occasion throughout the action of the play, and their recurring presence helps to destroy our ordinary sense of chronology. In this play time is so foreshortened as to cease to exist. Much less than *Tamburlaine* or *Edward II* or even *The Jew of Malta*, this play has little sense of sequence. It is as though the full action occurs in a flash, as though all the twenty-four years for which Faustus contracts are expended in an instant. As in a dream, cause and effect exist simultaneously. The recurring Good and Bad Angels help make the beginning and the end seem instantaneous. Marlowe is not concerned with crime and punishment, which is, necessarily, a temporal matter. He is concerned with the state of Faustus' soul, an eternal matter, outside time. Faustus' actions only illustrate its turmoil; they are not the cause of turmoil.

The stage action throughout the play is calculated to dramatize the themes of the play. When Valdes and Cornelius are brought to Faustus immediately following his initial, defining soliloquy, we learn that they have enticed him to magic and that they hope to use him for their own purposes. Having taught him the damning black arts, they hope to profit parasitically from his conjuring. Their kind of calculated evil is prudential, and human; but Faustus' conduct is of a different order altogether. The two kinds of

Talkes about Cornelius & Valdes

scholars are dramaturgically pitted against each other to show the qualities of two kinds of learning. In this respect, Faustus is committed to what we would call "pure scholarship"; Valdes and Cornelius to "applied scholarship." For Faustus, the search for knowledge is good in its own right; it need not be directed to human needs or have an absolute value. Faustus is ravished by his fantasy of total knowledge: "How am I glutted with conceit of this!" he says (I.i. 79). A megalomaniac for whom nothing exists but his will, he wants to engorge, to surround, all the universe together. In contrast, Valdes and Cornelius are worldly men; and, as bargainers, they want worldly reward at lowest cost. If Faustus is a scientist aspiring to be god, they are engineers, content to be human. Marlowe presents, on stage, two attitudes toward knowledge.

In the next scene we meet two other scholars who are uncorrupted by ambition. They know their limitations, and they mourn for Faustus. If Valdes and Cornelius define Faustus' position, these two heighten our awareness of his danger. And Wagner, his servant, demonstrates the essential irrationality of his actions. As Professor Bevington has recently observed, Wagner "makes a humorous application of the sophistry and syllogistic arguments of his learned master" (p. 253). Bevington has noted that from the beginning Marlowe establishes an alternating pattern of high drama and comic parody. The comedy of the clowns—the scene with the scholars and Wagner is only the first of several—keeps Faustus' actions in perspective. Their actions constantly make us aware of the ludicrousness of Faustus' aspiration. These humorous interludes are not gratuitous, grafted-on second thoughts but thematically and dramatically necessary to the basic concept of the play, in the same way that Valdes and Cornelius are necessary to it. The humorous episodes illustrate the limits of Faustus' nature. From the start the drama is "greatly planned," as Goethe says, both to investigate ideas and to stage them.

The next two scenes (I.iii, iv.) are paired; the stage movement from scene to scene was of course unbroken on the open Elizabethan stage. Wagner's conversation with the scholars (I.ii) was carried on in ordinary daylight, but now the stage is darkened so that Faustus may conjure. The stage directions are unusually complete: thunder is called for, and Lucifer and four devils—

"above" presumably, on the upper stage—observe the magic incantations.[13] Their presence suggests that they have been lying in
wait for Faustus, looking for an opportunity to leap on him. We
are to understand that Lucifer is at every man's elbow, awaiting
a misstep. Marlowe's world seems ringed round with dangers;
and life seems a perilous journey—a forgiving Christ is much
more remote than enticing devils. This whole scene is calculated
to give a shiver of horror, filled as it is with flash powder and
offstage noise. The spectacle is the dramatic equivalent of the
dialogue; it reinforces the theme with shows.

This episode, Act I, scene iii, may be the most fully conceived
of the play. It begins on a darkened stage with Faustus invoking
the night. We can imagine the sensation of Mephistophilis' first
appearance, for he comes suddenly, in thunder, following Faustus' Latin incantations. He has horns, cloven feet, and the tail
of the conventional red devil; he carries a fork and he leers. He
was no parody to the devil-fearing Elizabethans, but the standard
representation of God's antagonist. When Faustus immediately
sends Mephistophilis back to Hell to find a more pleasing shape,
such action is characteristic of him, as Kirschbaum has suggested,
for Faustus cannot accept things as they are; he must always
coat the ugly o'er with sugar.[14] The devil comes a second time as
"an old Franciscan friar." Friars may have had a devilish reputation in England for two hundred years, but at least they had
human form. The remainder of the scene defines Faustus' arrogant naïveté, his "aspiring pride and insolence" (I.iii. 68). He
paradoxically denies the existence of the truth which his senses
affirm, the very senses which he now sells his soul to gratify.

In the subsequent exchange Faustus questions his servant-devil
—he seems to think of him as a kind of Aladdin-genie[15]—and his
cockiness is contrasted to Mephistophilis' tragic grief in what is
indeed a bold dramatic stroke. We can hardly pass over the
depth of Mephistophilis' bitter regret as he repeats the name of
Lucifer in their exchange:

> FAUSTUS: And what are you that live with Lucifer?
> MEPHISTOPHILIS: Unhappy spirits that fell with Lucifer,
> Conspired against our God with Lucifer,
> And are for ever damned with Lucifer. (I.iii. 70–73)

This devil suffers from a despair so great that he becomes God's advocate, even as he recognizes himself as lost. Although the speech foretells Faustus' own end, Faustus is too proud to be taught; he thinks only of his own opinions. In great passion Mephistophilis indicates the spiritual nature of God's hell:

> FAUSTUS: How comes it then that thou art out of hell?
> MEPHISTOPHILIS: Why this is hell, nor am I out of it.
> Think'st thou that I who saw the face of God
> And tasted the eternal joys of heaven
> Am not tormented with ten thousand hells
> In being deprived of everlasting bliss?
> O Faustus, leave these frivolous demands
> Which strike a terror to my fainting soul.
>   (I.iii. 75–82)

There is no pain so great, Aesçhylus says, as the memory of joy in present grief. Frivolously, Faustus denies the existence of everything except the physical present, even while the eternal Mephistophilis stands before him. Faustus exhibits once more the pride that would measure all the universe by his human standard:

> What, is great Mephistophilis so passionate
> For being deprivèd of the joys of heaven?
> Learn thou of Faustus manly fortitude,
> And scorn those joys thou never shalt possess.
>   (I.iii. 83–86)

We are thus prepared for the exultation of his aria at the conclusion of the scene. It begins: "Had I as many souls as there be stars,/ I'd give them all for Mephistophilis" (I.iii. 102–03). Faustus has clearly not understood the "old philosophers" with whom he tries to associate himself. Socrates said that Knowledge is Virtue; but Faustus, with Bacon, discovers that Knowledge is Power.[16] Faustus has turned his back on the Christian universe, and he also rejects the Classical. In doing so, he is the first modern man.

There follows a companion scene with Wagner and the Clown (I.iv.) that reduces all the foregoing superhuman aspiration to human proportion. The sensual satisfaction for which the doctor yearns is now seen on a vulgar level. The corruption of these clowns is Faustus' responsibility; as the master is lost, so also is the servant. In bartering his own soul, Faustus endangers Wagner's and the others'. Although the clowns would sell their souls for a shoulder of mutton, if it be well roasted and have a good sauce, they are yet wiser than Faustus. They receive comprehensible, human rewards for their sale; and, even at that, they have to be tricked into the devil's service. Moreover, we know also that they are unsteady in their fidelity to hell. At the first opportunity they will escape to human repentance because their vanity does not keep them from changing their minds. In their weakness they can achieve, therefore, a salvation unavailable to Faustus in his strength.

In the first act of the play, then, Faustus is shown dramatically and rhetorically to be confident to the point of arrogance, his will corrupted beyond redemption. He selfishly seeks power and sensual satisfaction, not as a means of service either to God or to his fellows, but as ends in themselves. He alienates himself from men, society, and the world. He endangers all who associate with him, even his servant. Because Marlowe represents his condition in dramatic action as well as in words, the act has unity and contains a consistent view of Faustus, the man determined in his ambitions. Act I might be called "The Decision."

In Act II Faustus wavers, but he finally reaches a legal agreement with Mephistophilis—and Act II could well be called "The Contract." Faustus' second thoughts are reflected in stage action. The Good and Bad Angels appear:

> GOOD ANGEL: Sweet Faustus, think of heaven and
> heavenly things.
> BAD ANGEL: No Faustus; think of honor and wealth
> (II.i. 21–22)

In a magnificently theatrical and essentially comic scene—a comic scene without laughter because the issues are too great for laughter—Faustus and Mephistophilis conclude their agreement. In *Tamburlaine Part Two* Tamburlaine wounded himself in full view of the audience, gashing his arm that his blood might flow. When Faustus stabs himself for the blood with which to sign away his soul, Marlowe repeats the sensation. For all his professed skill in analytics, Faustus seems unaware that the devil cannot be bound by covenants and that he has thus become both spiritually and intellectually irresponsible. (Arthur Mizener suggests that Faustus is caught between medieval otherworldliness and Renaissance legality.[17]) Standing there in the darkness with Mephistophilis and his bleeding arm, Faustus hesitates, his spirit troubled, all his humanity in his irresolution. Quickly Mephistophilis calls up a glorious show; for, as Kirschbaum has observed, "Sensual pleasure is always Faustus' remedy for spiritual despair" (p. 237). According to Marlowe's stage directions, devils dance, wearing crowns and rich clothing; and the stage is filled with light, which we—if not Faustus—can recognize as the flickering fires of hell. The show having faded, Faustus is ridiculously reconciled to his deed of gift.

In the second half of this scene, Faustus claims his immediate reward: the full satisfaction of intellectual curiosity. He asks about the nature of hell and is not satisfied to learn that hell is a state of mind, so determined a materialist he has become. Unable to be content with answers which we and Mephistophilis recognize as true, Faustus calls for a wife, only to find that he must be satisfied with a courtesan. As a partner of hell, sacramental unions are unavailable to him; he must accept devilish substitutes. His range of activity is as circumscribed now as before. Earlier he could not rise to heavenly things, and he is less capable of doing so now.

The second scene of Act II is similar to the first in construction. Again Faustus hesitates over his decision in a speech which recalls his earlier declaration that, for Mephistophilis, he would give as many souls as there be stars (I.iii. 102ff):

> When I behold the heavens, then I repent
> And curse thee, wicked Mephistophilis,
> Because thou hast deprived me of those joys.
> (II.ii. 1–3)

As formerly he asked about the nature of hell, now he asks about heaven. "Let us dispute again," he says, "And reason of divine astrology" (II.ii. 33–34). The questions put and answered are deceptive. Faustus is not asking scientific questions though they are couched in what appears to be scientific language. He is really asking teleological questions; he does not want to know by what means the universe was constructed, but for what purpose, and to what use, it was made. Such questions cannot be answered, by Marlowe or anybody else; they are questions of faith, beyond Faustus' ratiocinative powers: this first modern man wants scientific answers to religious questions.

When Faustus presses, Mephistophilis thunders like the Voice out of the Whirlwind: "Think thou of hell." Man can be saved by faith alone, Mephistophilis says, becoming for the moment the Lord's advocate. Faustus, touched, nearly repents; but, as usual, he is treated to a spectacle, this time of the Seven Deadly Sins. Hardly one of the high poetic moments of the play, this scene relies on visual rather than aural effects. The great parade ends with Faustus' words: "O, how this sight doth delight my soul!" (II.ii. 163).

This spectacle is the greatest Faustus has yet seen, but others are to come. Hereafter, Faustus himself will be the impresario of sensual spectacle, managing the movement and delighting in the color. From the scholar searching for universal purpose in his library of ancient tomes, the learned doctor has now become the manager of night club divertissement. Act II, scene ii, ends with Lucifer giving Faustus a book from which to learn new entertainments, and in the usual parody scene that follows, the clowns with a book also prepare magic entertainments. In both scenes, the one vulgar, the other learned, the flesh and the spirit are united; the satisfaction of the body is accomplished by the exercise of the intellect. Both scenes deny that satisfactions differ in kind, that spiritual hunger cannot be quenched with cake; and in both the eye and the ear are alike filled.

III *The Second Part of* Faustus

Acts I and II—"The Decision" and "The Contract"—are a unit. They deal with Faustus' determination to satisfy his unqualified curiosity, and in them ultimate questions of purpose are raised but left unanswered. In Acts III and IV Faustus sheds the glory of his original quest and seems increasingly content to be only a magician. Like Macbeth, he has been coarsened by his ambition. The language through these acts is similarly coarse and uninteresting. Act III might be titled "The Challenge to Reli-

gious Power"; for, in it, Faustus goes to Rome where he sports
with the Pope—with a Pope who seems less worthy of admiration than Faustus himself. Marlowe disparages the theological
pretensions of the Pope and the philosophical pretensions of
Faustus. Act IV, which might be called "The Disintegration of
Power," takes Faustus from the center of religious authority to
the center of political authority, the court of the German Emperor. There, even more than at Rome, Faustus is reduced from
high metaphysical speculation to trickery. In the middle acts of
this play Faustus' imagination is in steady decline, and the
learned doctor is confined to smaller and smaller areas of influence. Prometheus has become Tyl Eulenspiegel.

The chorus introductory to Act III summarizes. Faustus, we
learn, has given up the study of astrology. Lucifer has not forbidden this investigation; as one critic has observed, "it is his
own evil will, which has already determined not to embrace the
truths to which astrology is leading."[18] He turns from a study of
the heavens to the study of this world, to geography; but infinity
cannot be comprehended on earth. Although years from physical
death, Faustus has already come to spiritual stagnation, his intellectual appetites satisfied with bonbons. Marlowe is faced with
a major task in this section of the play; on the philosophical-
religious aspect, he is obviously unable to answer Faustus' cosmological questions, but no man can answer them, except by
faith; and this Faustus rejects. The dramatic problem is how to
represent Faustus as powerful in person yet powerless in spirit.
Marlowe does this by showing Faustus substituting mechanical
frivolities for pure speculation.

In keeping with the spiritual and aspirational decline of Faustus, the quality of the verse weakens; in place of the poetry of
the first acts, Marlowe now provides spectacle; but what is lost
in language is compensated at least in part by dramatic variety.
When properly staged, the middle scenes of the play hold their
own very well indeed. Accounts of various recent productions
suggest some of the stage possibilities for these middle scenes
of the play. Faustus in Act III visits Rome, dressed sumptuously
as a cardinal—Mephistophilis asks, "Now tell me, Faustus, are we
not fitted well?" (III.i. 162)—and disrupts a papal banquet.
Michael Benthall, producer of the 1961 *Faustus* in Edinburgh,

exploited the visual possibilities in this scene. He realized, according to the London *Times* (August 23, 1961), "that if the trivial conjuring tricks are played in surroundings of much splendour they will gain enormously in importance. The open stage enables the necessary splendour to be achieved. . . . The scene is so impressive in its solemnity that almost any joke would seem tellingly out of place, and the final wrecking of all this grandeur by Faustus and Mephistophilis seems indeed a devilish outrage" (p. 11). Eric Keown, writing of the same scene in *Punch*, said that "the pageant of the interrupted papal meeting is staged with magnificence. The contrast between the fusty sobriety of Faustus's study and the riot of colour when he gets loose as a magician is extremely effective." He goes on to comment on the total effect of the spectacle in this production: "No production of it has ever before made me feel how terrifying an experience it must have been for the audiences for which it was written, to whom the pains of hell and the anguish of a doomed soul were so much more real than they are in this slipshod age."[19] In not relying on his "mighty line" in these acts Marlowe does not, therefore, impoverish his play as scholars in their studies have thought; he exploits the theater.

Moreover these non-verbal scenes have thematic implications. The Pope is a kind of worsened Faustus, for, in him, hypocrisy is added to ambition. Both men try to manipulate religion for worldly purpose, but the Pope is less powerful than Faustus. He can tread on the neck of the German Frederick to show that "all power on earth [is] bestowed on us" (III.i. 152), but he cannot protect himself from Faustus' pranks. He damns his tormentor, not knowing that Faustus is already damned. The scene ends in a travesty of religious form: Faustus is cursed as a witch with bell, book, and candle for possessing power not subject to the Pope's control. And Act III ends with yet another parody; for, after the Friars chant the office of excommunication, the clowns burlesque Faustus' disruption of the papal court. In the most spectacular of the play's comic scenes, to their stupefaction they conjure up Mephistophilis himself. Throughout Act III Marlowe's dramaturgical technique is the same as that used in Acts I and II: each scene consists of contrasting variations on its central idea.

In Act IV, "The Disintegration of Power," [Marlowe first takes Faustus to the imperial capital of Charles V; and thereby turns from religion to politics. In his original dealings with Mephistophilis, Faustus has initiated cosmic questions; in his dealings with the Pope, he engaged in satirical horse play; and now he is little more than a court juggler. The gorgeous pretensions of papal Rome have given place to the games of Germany. Famous for his "learned skill," Faustus answers any chance questioner, and does parlor tricks. For the pleasure of the Emperor, he calls up the ghosts of Alexander and Darius, and for sport he horns and unhorns the lesser nobility. As Faustus descends to greater vulgarity, Marlowe gives us dramatized devil-lore; and the vulgar folk-activities have more than a touch of Marlovian sadism. Benvolio, threatening Faustus, says: "We'll put out his eyes, and they shall serve for buttons to his lips to keep his tongue from catching cold" (IV.iii. 63–64). In another place Faustus casts Benvolio and his colleagues into "lowest hell" after certain physical abuse. In the second episode of Act IV Faustus abuses a horse-courser in even more vulgar spirit. The old separation of scholar from servant has collapsed, and the learned doctor and the peasants have become of a single kind. Faustus' dramatic descent from comprehending the stars to teasing Robin has been visual, orderly, and complete. Its success depends on the elaborate business implied in the lines and stage directions.

[The concluding act of the play returns Faustus to his post of learned dignity] and the verse is as eloquent here as it was in Acts I and II. [Act V, which might be titled "The Reckoning," begins with yet one more spectacle—devils like waiters parade across the stage carrying the materials of a final feast—and with a summarizing prologue spoken by Wagner:

> I think my master means to die shortly.
> He hath made his will and given me his wealth,
> His house, his goods, and store of golden plate,
> Besides two thousand ducats ready coined.
> I wonder what he means. If death were nigh,
> He would not frolic thus. He's now at supper . . .
>   (V.i. 1–6)

As usual, in the face of disaster Faustus quiets his apprehensions with frolic. In the first four acts we have learned that, when a

[84]

man forgets that the proper study of mankind is not God but man, or when a man tries to measure the universe to his own specifications, he becomes fit companion for clowns.

In this concluding act Faustus still suffers from pride, but it is now guised as despair. Faustus thinks that God himself cannot save him, so mighty a sinner he is, and he rejects the grace of God. Even in his extremity he learns nothing, and he remains legalistic to the end. He thinks that what is contracted must be paid, what is ordered must be delivered; and, between the deed and the reward, he recognizes no mercy. An Old Man instructs him to the contrary:

> Though thou has now offended like a man,
> Do not persevere in it like a devil.
> Yet, yet, thou hast an amiable soul,
> If sin by custom grow not into nature.
>   (V.i. 41–44)

Faustus despairs, although an angel hovers o'er his head "with a vial full of precious grace" (V.i. 62). He is one of those unhappy souls who cherishes his faults like merits. He is the ultimate romantic individualist, for he prefers to assert himself and be damned than to submit and be saved. He would rather rule in hell than serve in heaven, not realizing that ruling in hell is also serving. Faustus repeats his early commitment to Lucifer and then, with the full malice of his fallen nature, asks punishment for the Old Man who has just tempted him to salvation. He says to Mephistophilis:

> Torment, sweet friend, that base and agèd man
> That durst dissuade me from thy Lucifer,
> With greatest torment that our hell affords.
>   (V.i. 84–86)

But the devil cannot touch the Old Man because his faith is too great. And once more Faustus "gluts" his appetite to deaden his quickened apprehension: Helen passes over the stage between two cupids—

> Was this the face that launched a thousand ships
> And burnt the topless towers of Ilium?
> Sweet Helen, make me immortal with a kiss. [She kisses him.]
> Her lips suck forth my soul. See where it flies!

Come, Helen, come, give me my soul again.
Here will I dwell, for heaven is in these lips,
And all is dross that is not Helena.   (V.i. 99–105)

This celebrated passage contains the precision of diction and
reference which we have noted in the language of Acts I and II.
The voice rises at the end of each line as always with Marlowe,
suggesting the open aspiration of the speaker for limitless regions.

When he embraces Helen, Faustus is finally lost. The Old Man
tells us so, and we must believe him. Greg has proposed that
the unforgivable sin which Faustus commits is cohabitation with
spirits, this Helen being but the spirit of Homer's Helen;[20] but
this interpretation may be too explicit. Instead, Helen is a kind
of pagan Virgin Mary, an Anti-Mary, as it were; and, in seeking
Helen's embrace, Faustus rejects the guardian of the Church's
store of Grace, the Virgin Mary. He accepts in place of Mary a
phantom, a dream of pagan beauty, the shadow of a world his-
torically and permanently lost. Spengler observed how late in
medieval times the Mary-cult of prayer and the Devil-cult of
spells developed together: "Man walked continuously on the
thin crust of the bottomless pit. Life in this world [was] a cease-
less and desperate contest with the Devil."[21] The Tragical History of Doctor Faustus grows from these Devil-cults, and Hel-
en's worldly sensuousness is the antithesis of the Virgin's sacred
purity.

Boas complains that Marlowe never gives us a glimpse of
Faustus in his sinful pleasure and suggests that Goethe was
wiser "when he exhibited his Faust as the seducer of the simple
maiden, Gretchen."[22] But Faustus' sin is spiritual, and it can only
be expressed spiritually. His fault lies not so much in the nature
of his doing as in the nature of his being. Marlowe strives always
to present his spiritual state without diluting it into a limiting
action. He is not saying that Faustus is damned for a single deed
or series of deeds; he is saying that Faustus is damned because
of his corrupted nature. His nature allows him to prefer Helen
to Mary, and his nature profanes his every act.

[86]

Faustus' destiny hangs entirely on his faith. The Old Man's final words explain why he is saved and Faustus lost:

> Satan begins to sift me with his pride.
> As in this furnace God shall try my faith,
> My faith, vile hell, shall triumph over thee.
> Ambitious fiends, see how the heavens smiles
> At your repulse and laughs your state to scorn.
> Hence hell, for hence I fly unto my God.   (V.i. 122–27)

Faustus has now come to the moment of death, a moment anticipated through the full length of the play, and Marlowe uses all the dramaturgical techniques which he has formerly exploited.

Faustus' first soliloquy in the first act was a kind of "argument" for the drama, and this last scene begins with a corresponding summary. Again it is night in Faustus' study, and the doctor wears the plain academic robe of the first act—a garment which contrasts with the splendor of the cardinal and imperial dress of Acts III and IV. In his first dealings with Lucifer, Faustus was observed from above (I.iii.); now, in his final agonies, Lucifer, Beëlzebub and Mephistophilis look down on him again. But only Mephistophilis, his usual companion, speaks. The rest wait, their presence suggesting the mystery of what now takes place.

Dying, Faustus tries to settle his human accounts. First, we see him with Wagner; and realize that the old relationship of master and servant has returned since Faustus concerns himself with his inferior's welfare. Next, we see him once more with his fellow scholars. During this conversation, Faustus, like Macbeth, sees apparitions. He swings almost hysterically from a calm, perhaps proud, acceptance of his damnation to encompassing terror: "Ah, my sweet chamber-fellow, had I lived with thee, then had I lived still, but now must die eternally," he says. And then, when Mephistophilis approaches, he leans into the arms of his friends and screams: "Look, sirs; comes he not? Comes he not?" (V.ii. 28–30). Never before has Faustus had such fellow-feeling. In his extremity he turns to human love; but, as Fellowship could not accompany Everyman into his grave, so the three scholars cannot go with their friend to his death. Prudently they withdraw and Faustus is dramatically alone.

With human uncertainty and a hint of animal vigor, Faustus prays that his fears be groundless, that the world be as senseless as he had assumed. Even in his extremity he asserts himself; for as Mephistophilis approaches, Faustus says: "O thou bewitching fiend, 'twas thy temptation/ Hath robbed me of eternal happiness (V.ii. 87–88). But this is a distortion of the situation, for Faustus had importuned the fiend, not the fiend Faustus. For the last time the Good and Bad Angels appear, but they no longer urge repentance; instead, the Good Angel brings a vision of what Faustus has lost. With music, the throne of heaven descends, surrounded by its choirs of faithful souls. This Cimabue heaven is all gold with "those bright shining saints" (V.ii. 109) and recalls medieval painting which lacks perspective. This vision is replaced by one of Hell, a "vast perpetual torture-house" (V.ii. 114), flame-red and black, too horrible to look upon—and it reminds us of the paintings of Hieronimus Bosch. Faustus averts his eyes. His torture has begun. The stage has vividly presented the contrasting modes of the play.

Faustus' final soliloquy has been often and justly praised. In it, time is foreshortened as it has been throughout the drama. Like the twenty-four years, this last hour passes like a dream, flaming out in a single instant. Moreover, this speech gathers up the imagery and ideas of the whole play. Its references to the stars recall both the cosmic questions with which Faustus' restlessness began and the price he offered to pay: "Had I as many souls as there be stars . . ." (I.iii. 102). His yearning for the redeeming blood of Christ recalls his own blood-oath with Mephistophilis. Even at this moment of death he clings to his rational conception of a universe in which God, Lucifer, and himself are bound by legal arrangements. Faustus cannot conceive of God as wiser or larger or more merciful; to the very last moment of his earthly existence, Faustus measures life by human specifications. And then at last he turns on the world for which he has sold his soul: he wishes that he had never been born or, if born, created a brutish beast; he forswears the humanity which he has exalted; and, in his agony, he tries to regress to the world before books, to a world before thought. In thunder the observing fiends approach and the concluding "Ah, Mephistophilis!" is cried in total darkness.

[88]

Only a double coda remains. Faustus' faithful friends find his limbs, torn and scattered, and we are reminded of the comic disembowelment of Faustus by the horse-coursers (IV.v.). Dawn light is replaced by full flat illumination:

> Cut is the branch that might have grown full straight,
> And burnèd is Apollo's laurel bough
> That sometime grew within this learnèd man. . . .
>
> (Epilogue 1–3)

In the archaic morality plays from which *The Tragical History of Doctor Faustus* descends, Mankind was saved. These liturgical plays were comedies, for they ended happily in that they illustrated the redeeming love of God in a world of man-made chaos. Marlowe's morality play is not a comedy, for in it God is remote; his love does not redeem Faustus, and the drama does not settle Faustus' questions. No medieval play of Christian faith, this dramatizes the modern tragic view of the universe in which the tragic hero "goes out no craven sinner but violently, speaking the rage and despair of all mankind who would undo the past."[23] When the play ends, we are asked neither by the scholars nor by the chorus to hold Faustus in contempt. We come away from this play with a sense less of the justice of the universe than of its incomprehensible irrationality.

Faustus, like Tamburlaine, is obsessed with power. In *Tamburlaine* Marlowe saw his hero as superior to the gods; the gods are as ineffectual in this play as they had been in *Dido, Queen of Carthage*. But in *The Tragical History of Doctor Faustus* celestial power is no longer contemptible; on the contrary, it is very great indeed. But, if the forces of Good and Evil are great, Faustus as the aspiring human doctor has his nobility too. The grandeur of heaven does not reduce this intellectual voyager to insignificance. This play repeats Marlowe's principal themes—his fascination with power, his glory in the physical world, his admiration for human grandeur. In their dramatic combination these themes speak to us directly, and Faustus catches our imagination; for Faustus is ourselves. Like Faustus in the sixteenth century, we in the twentieth are fascinated with the exercise of power; we hedge our petty sovereignties with atomic weapons; we exploit all nature for our physical satisfactions; and we cockily determine to remake the world to our specifications. Faustus and the modern who finds no limit to a scientific inquiry are the same man. It is not odd that a generation which willingly expends its wealth of matter and spirit to get to the moon and beyond, claiming curiosity as the one human quality not subject to rational, purposive restraint—it is not odd that this is the generation which returns to Faustus. Perhaps it is because his end haunts our dreams.

CHAPTER 5

Theatricalism in The Jew of Malta *and* The Massacre at Paris

I *The Problems of* The Jew

MARLOWE MUST HAVE WRITTEN *The Jew of Malta* shortly after his success with *Tamburlaine*. The Prologue to *The Jew* links that play to *The Massacre at Paris*, or, as Henslowe characteristically named it in his theatrical diary of the 1590's, *The Guise*. The Prologue of *The Jew* begins:

> Albeit the world think Machiavel is dead,
> Yet was his soul but flown beyond the Alps,
> And, now the Guise is dead. . .   (Prol. 1–3)

The Machiavellian Barabas, the chief character in *The Jew*, is thus explicitly associated with the Machiavellian Guise, the most fascinating character in *The Massacre*. Guise and Barabas both maintain that "might first made kings," that laws are most sure when "they were writ in blood," and that religion is "but a child-ish toy." Of the two, Guise is the more perfect exemplar of

Machiavellian doctrine because he aspires to political authority and even identifies himself with Caesar; but both plays deal with rebels in political situations.

The dates of the two plays are not certain, but 1589 or 1590 cannot be far wrong for *The Jew*. The title role was played by Edward Alleyn, the leading actor of the day, and it was an immediate success. It remained the most popular of Marlowe's plays on the stage; and perhaps for this reason was not published until 1633. This 1633 text, our only source for the play, is full of errors; it shows unmistakable signs of revision, probably by Thomas Heywood, an industrious literary journeyman and dramatist of the time. Written in the chronological middle of his career, *The Jew of Malta* is a benchmark in Marlowe's development and is an important play for several reasons; it exhibits the direction of his growth, and, in addition, it had a notable influence on Marlowe's greatest contemporaries.

The Jew of Malta is closely related to Shakespeare's *Merchant of Venice* (1596?). Both playwrights deal with scheming Jews who live in alien societies—both Shylock and Barabas have fair daughters who love Gentiles, both are moved to revenge by an extraordinary animus. With its beautiful, imprisoned damsel and its ogre, *The Merchant of Venice* is a romance that skirts tragedy. The ogre, as it turns out, is more than a fairy tale villain—his passions are as real as a pogrom—but Shakespeare's is an enchanted world. Marlowe's is not; his is a world bewitched. *The Jew of Malta* is bloody, violent, and coarse; and oddly enough, it is also funny—it is a comedy that approaches melodrama. Neither so romantic as Shakespeare's play nor so vivid, it might have come from the Brothers Grimm.

The Jew of Malta may also have been a source of inspiration for Jonson's *Volpone, or The Fox* (1606). In both *Volpone* and *The Jew* an Italianate villain maneuvers his avaricious abusers into disaster, aided and abetted by a "parasite" who ultimately turns on him. In both plays the chief schemer is at last enmeshed in his own machinations. Both plays are farcical; both touch upon the repugnant and yet achieve gaiety. But unlike Jonson, Marlowe strikes us as essentially innocent and his play as unfinished. Marlowe lacks Jonson's understanding of moral complexity, and he lacks Jonson's high artistic patina. As Alfred Harbage has shrewdly observed, the Jew's range of depravity is limited. Although Barabas kills people "in heaps," he is most remiss in administering mental or physical agony. Professor Harbage continues: "The heady combination of lust and bloodshed, eroticism *cum* the macabre" to be found in Webster and Middleton and in Jonson "does not appear in *The Jew of Malta*."[1] Compared to Volpone, who is a connoisseur of Italianate sensualism, Barabas is a country boy. When Marlowe wrote *The Jew of Malta*, he had not yet outgrown a rather adolescent desire to shock his audience with cynical views of Christianity and with staged violence. His audiences were much less sophisticated than the Jacobeans, and he did not try to titillate them as later playwrights could and did.

Marlowe was unsophisticated in another way. The motives and reactions in *The Jew* are not thoroughly consistent, for its heavy debt to the old-fashioned morality drama has been incompletely digested. Like them its characters are not psychologically of a piece, nor are the implications of individual passages fully considered. Indeed, Marlowe sustains no single unifying attitude throughout the whole play. As a result, contrary to what T. S. Eliot says, the play is not everywhere "terribly serious" nor always very "savage," but is, rather, sensational comedy which sometimes touches deeper notes.[2] L. C. Knights has suggested that though the play at times is "serious farce"—he is trading on Eliot's provocative phrase "tragic farce"—at other times it "becomes something like an undergraduate parody of a play that had yet to be written."[3] Altogether the play is spotty, its purposes inconstantly and inconsistently realized.

In tone, then, *The Jew of Malta* is a jumble, but its overall plotting is brilliantly conceived for theatrical effect. If inconsistently executed, the dramatic relation of one episode to another is "greatly planned."[4] It is easy to guess why the play is so uneven—that is, how it came to be a play primarily of momentary effects. Hurrying to exploit the fame that he had recently won with *Tamburlaine*, Marlowe seized on the sensational folk-story of the Jew of Malta; but after blocking out the action and before he could give detailed shape to his material, his interests became engaged elsewhere. What is true of *The Jew of Malta* is, in more or less degree, true of all that Marlowe wrote—he conceived boldly and executed carelessly.

II   The Jew of Malta

For all its uneven tone, in dramaturgical outline *The Jew* is clear and divides itself into two quite equal parts. The first section ends with Act III, scene iii, the climax of the play—up to this point Barabas has held the initiative. Thereafter he goes on the defensive, responding ingeniously to challenge but starting nothing; only in Act V, scenes ii and iii, does he again manage the action. The incidents of the play are arranged so that what happens in the first half prepares for what happens in the second; and as is common in well-made plays, the action comes full circle.

Act I is the most carefully sustained section of the whole play; for in it theme, action, and tone are most fully matched. The opening prologue seems to announce ideas which will give unity to a variety of incident. Machiavelli, as the Prologue, proclaims that he has many friends in England who "weigh not men, and therefore not men's words" (1). An atheist, he holds that "might first made kings" (2) and that strong citadels support kings better than authority or love. In a religious century, he is not merely unreligious but anti-religious, and he prepares us for Barabas, whom we meet in the first scenes of the play. Marlowe intends us to see that Barabas, like Machiavelli, denies the validity of the Christian verities, that he is to be hated and feared for this reason, and that he is dealing in blood as a consequence of his dangerous beliefs. These beliefs are the root cause of his threat, and the action of Act I shadows forth this Machiavellianism.

Like Machiavelli, Barabas embraces the only apparent alternative to Christian faith, Satan's code of reasonable self-assertion, and he swears "i' the devil's name!" (I.ii.155). In his pride he measures human action by its benefit to himself. Power becomes the only value worthy of striving for; and the means to power, Barabas and Machiavelli assert, is wealth. Like Faustus, they are both confident that religion sets up no valid barriers to their ambitions. It is important to recognize that Machiavelli and Barabas suffer from perverted wills, but that the road to salvation remains open to them—they can always embrace the true faith. Barabas is thus an infidel;[5] he is not a member of a doomed, inferior race which bears inalienable, contaminated blood. Barabas, like Machiavelli, is a persistent unbeliever; the disbelieving Jew and the apostate Italian are of a kind.

The modern view of Judaism differs from this Renaissance view. In modern times it is impossible for a Jew to become a Christian because he is "scientifically" a Jew—that is, his identity is determined by his genes, not his beliefs. According to modern pseudo-scientific thought, the Jewish "race" has no entrance and no exit, but the Elizabethan Barabas is a Jew by a conscious act of continuing rejection, and his will, not his "blood," is corrupt. When Abigail, Barabas' daughter, recognizes the falseness of her father's faith, she is converted and escapes censure. That she was raised in a tradition that has steadfastly maintained its anti-Christian identity makes her acceptance of Christian truth notable, but it does not make it impossible. Unlike Abigail and like Machiavelli, Barabas remains in darkness though he has been shown the light. Embracing evil knowingly, he is a lost soul.

Barabas is, then, a rebel, as romantically independent as Faustus and Tamburlaine. Shakespeare's Shylock is quite different, for he is no revolutionary. The Jew of Venice cleverly turns the laws of Venice to his own advantage—"If you deny me, fie upon your law!" Shylock says to the Venetian court (IV.i.101)—but Barabas constructs new law as he goes along because he must live outside legal restrictions. Shakespeare's Jew is presented with several possible legal alternatives to his chosen line of revenge, but Marlowe's Jew is offered nothing of the kind. If Barabas is to survive, he must survive in spite of society, independent of its regulations; he is more abused than Shylock because more firmly trapped, and he is less interesting because less complicated in his reactions. Nonetheless, throughout this first act our attention has been vigorously engaged by his acrobatic superiority to conventional Malta; a villain, Barabas yet earns some of our admiration.

In Act I, if not in the rest of the play, the Machiavellian ideas

of the Prologue are reflected in stage action. The opening theatrical scenes show us the conduct typical of one who suffers
from a diseased will. In Act I, scene i, we break in on the middle
of Barabas' meditations; he has a sheaf of papers—bills of lading,
receipts, and orders—in his hands; and we see him turn from
them to "paltry silverlings," which he discards as trash. As F. P.
Wilson says, "the movement and gestures of the actor are suggested in every line" of this opening speech.[6] Barabas appears
to be the center of commercial authority, and one critic has
cleverly suggested that he "adumbrates the capitalist" because
his satisfaction comes "less by possession than by control."[7]
Barabas is the greatest of what in later, capitalistic centuries we
identify as "robber barons." He is concerned with power and
with money as a means to it.

The nature of this independent entrepreneur is defined in action on stage by the persons who come to see him. First we
learn from two Jewish merchants of Barabas' prominence and
his superiority in Malta. Barabas has no more feeling for his
brothers in Judaism than he has for the Maltese, for his Jewish
faith is not really an issue in the play; it is used metaphorically
—to separate Barabas from all other men. One of Marlowe's soli-
tary heroes, his Judaism emphasizes his determined isolation.
"Howe'er the world go, I'll make sure for one," he says (I.i. 184).

In the first scene Marlowe goes to some lengths to establish
the fact that Barabas is the cleverest, the most unscrupulous,
the richest, and therefore the most powerful merchant in Chris-
tendom. This having been made clear, all the major plots (except one) can be introduced by the end of scene ii. Quickly and
fully we learn of the Turkish threat, of the Maltese determination to force the Jews to pay for their security, of Barabas' daughter who is so dutiful that she will perjure herself at his command,
of the lascivious friars who eye her, and of Lodowick and Mathias
who love her. We also learn that it takes more than the Maltese
Ferneze to best Barabas. Although Malta confiscates his goods,
he will yet be rich. This first act is a model of exposition and
preliminary suspense, for no detail is introduced that does not
lead directly to subsequent action.

Act I has an admirable unity, but from the very beginning of
Act II, theme, character, and action are less well combined. In

the earlier plays spectacle was used poetically, to carry symbolic meaning; but after Act I of *The Jew* stage action is introduced for its own sake, for the delight of the moment, with little overriding consideration of its relevance to an informing concept, and as a result the Jew's speeches seem strangely unrelated to one another. One critic has observed that Barabas' first speech (II.i. 1–19) is "lighted with scriptural grandeur"; at this moment he is "no Atheist, but an anti-Christian praying to the wrathful deity of his tribe, a prophet imprecating the avenging Jehovah."[8] And yet within fifty lines he has become a Punch and Judy puppet, clasping in ludicrous rapture the bags of gold thrown to him by his daughter—Abigail has pretended to take religious vows in order to reach and return Barabas' money.

The tone is startlingly inconsistent, and we hardly know how to square Barabas' celebrated confession to Ithamore in scene iii with what we already know of him. The speech begins:

> As for myself, I walk abroad 'a nights
> And kill sick people groaning under walls.
> Sometimes I go about and poison wells,
> And now and then, to cherish Christian thieves,
> I am content to lose some of my crowns
> That I may, walking in my gallery,
> See 'em go pinioned along by my door. . . .
> (II.iii. 171–77)

The extravagance of this brag reduces it to the level of schoolboy prank, and we laugh at its adolescent audacity. Some have tried to justify the speech dramatically by seeing Barabas as testing his newly purchased slave.[9] Others have thought the speech was "clearly made for laughter," that it is "conceived with the exotic relish and cruel humor of Nashe" in a kind of "extravagant comic villainy."[10] The speech is a puzzle, for it suggests a general malevolence not supported by Barabas' other activities; throughout the play, Barabas harms others only for revenge or for gain. This speech is thematically and psychologically irrelevant because it is unsynthesized into a total view of the Jew. It is a purple passage and its own excuse for existence; the play is full of such things.

The action of Act II develops what was initiated in Act I, and it prepares for what is to be developed in Acts III and IV; but the emphasis of Act II is on momentary effects. In Act III we see the same inconsistent theatricality we saw in Act II. It used to be said that *The Jew* breaks down thematically and dramatically at the end of Act II. H. S. Bennett's opinion is representative: ". . . towards the end of the second act this controlling power seems to fail and we are fobbed off with two acts of vastly inferior drama."[11]

But some students find a greater uniformity in Acts II, III, and IV than this observation suggests. Although the tempo of the action increases in Act III, Marlowe's careful attention to general structure and his carelessness in detail are what we have seen before. Indeed, all the action of the later parts of the play have been carefully anticipated, and the new persons of the third act—Bellamira, the courtesan, and Pilia-Borza, her procurer —have the kind of theatrical vitality and wit that the Jews and merchants of the earlier acts had. Bellamira is a vulgar, feminine variation of Barabas himself; like him she aspires beyond silver. When first we met him, Barabas called silver "trash" (I.i.7) and when we first meet her, she also disdains it (III.i.13). Both attempt to fish in troubled waters, and both cooperate with their opponents in order to use them. Both study "policy"—expediency. Barabas' ambitions reach beyond avarice to power, and Bellamira's stop with gold; but both have assistants, both are involved in love plots, and both have a vividness beyond the requirements of the action.

The second half of the play is like the first half in yet another important respect. The potentially tragic situations in it are again treated summarily or comically, and what might have had significance is glossed over. The tone remains uncertain. The scene, for example, in which Mathias and Lodowick kill each other is finished in thirty-five lines, and the comment by the bereaved parents is hardly more than perfunctory. When Abigail defects to Christianity, Barabas poisons all the inmates of her convent, as well as his own daughter, but the ludicrousness and horror of this act are not brought forward; we hardly know how we are supposed to react. Even Abigail's death is robbed of possible significance. In that scene (III.iv.) the friars' lecherous complaint that she died a virgin reduces the occasion to farce, and we find ourselves eager to see how quickly the friars will reveal what they have learned from her deathbed confession. Throughout the play Marlowe seems to have been satisfied to construct a theatrical entertainment and to explore its meaning only erratically.

Act IV is dramaturgically among the most brilliant sections of the play, but it is as uneven in tone as the rest. In it Marlowe provides a series of farcical tricks of the kind used before; Barabas, like a cat, always lands on his feet. When the act begins, Barabas learns that the friars know that he has poisoned the convent (IV.i.26), and he is thus clearly on the defensive. A series of funny exchanges ends with his famous lines:

> Fornication? But that
> Was in another country, and besides
> The wench is dead.   (IV.i. 41–43)

Barabas staves off any accusation by the Friars and then cleverly sets them against one another, exposing their avarice, which is as great as his own. In the next scene he and Ithamore permanently silence one of the friars by strangling him, and we laugh at Barabas' ingenuity. The corpse is propped up "as if he were begging of bacon" (IV.ii. 26), and it is struck down—"killed"—a moment later by his rival for Barabas' money, Friar Jacomo. The cheater, who was about to be cheated, has after all remained the master of the situation. Ithamore blandly observes that ". . . holy friars turn devils and murder one another" (IV.iii. 32–33). The first three scenes of Act IV have something in common with a Marx Brothers farce. The Marx Brothers, like Barabas and Ithamore, approached the sadistic when they abused their opponents; but, through it all, like Barabas, they rarely lost their audience. Barabas and Ithamore use Marx Brothers tricks in a mad world of violence and politics.

The second half of Act IV contains the kind of farcical reversal that we have seen before, and Barabas triumphs over a new set of opponents. Just as the friars attempted to acquire the Jew's money by converting him, Bellamira now attempts to get his money by blackmailing him. Bellamira pretends a passion for Ithamore and, when he makes love to her, the speeches are parodies of conventional love addresses. Ithamore says:

> I'll be Adonis; thou shalt be Love's queen.

The meads, the orchards, and the primrose lanes,
Instead of sedge and reed, bear sugar canes.
Thou in those groves, by Dis above,
Shalt live with me, and be my love. (IV. iv. 90–94)

"*Sugar cane!*" Professor Harbage says, "it is as if one were invoking the fleshly delights of peanut-brittle." The brothel in
which the scene takes place is "about as sexy as surgery" (p. 55).
We are not surprised when, in the next scene, Barabas turns the
tables on his enamored parasite and Bellamira. In dealing with
the friars, Barabas had pretended to be a penitent infidel (IV. i.);
now he pretends to be a French musician (IV. vi.). When he
appears disguised at Ithamore's drunken orgy—the orgy is about
as orgiastic as a Sunday School picnic—we must imagine his
ludicrous appearance. Any actor playing the part must have an
enormous nose and bear the trappings of a French musician.
Tuning his lute, Barabas speaks with a French accent laid over
his Jewish manner. (Did this scene suggest Volpone's mounte-
bank scene [II.ii.] to Jonson?) Barabas commands the situation.
For the second time in this act, the master cheater overcomes
his opponents.

The farcical reversals of Act IV continue in the concluding
act of the play. Act V begins with Bellamira's revelation to Ferneze of Barabas' murderous deeds. Very quickly the Jew is
seized, and more quickly he is given up for dead; but he is not
yet conquered:

> No, no.
> I drank of poppy and cold mandrake juice,
> And being asleep, belike they thought me dead
> And threw me o'er the walls. So—or how else—
> The Jew is here and rests at your command.
> (V.i. 77–81)

Barabas will not stay dead, any more than Falstaff or the figures
in a Punch and Judy show. He shares with them something of
the eternal Adam, and we cheer his resurrection. Within forty
lines he has overcome his Christian opponents, and once more
action has triumphed over verisimilitude, characterization, and
meaning.

But the Jew, though now the governor of Malta and supported

by the Turks, is not satisfied. He overextends himself, and the reversal is reversed. He says:

> . . . loving neither, will I live with both [Turks and Christian],
> Making a profit of my policy,
> And he from whom my most advantage comes
> Shall be my friend.   (V. ii. 111–14)

Barabas sells his allegiance to the highest bidder: "This is the life we Jews are used to lead—/ And reason too, for Christians do the like" (V. ii. 115–16). As *The Jew of Malta* continues, the tempo has so increased that any signification of theme must be ignored. In our studies we can discover the usual Marlovian disparagement of Christians, but on the stage the Christians and Jews all seem tarred with the same stick. They are all concerned with the narrowest self-interest.

The last farcical scene of the play fully exploits the machinery of the stage.[12] According to Marlowe's stage directions, Barabas is seen in the gallery of the stage "with a hammer, above, very busy" preparing a trap through which the Turkish forces are to be dropped. At the last moment, however, the Jew himself is plunged into the prepared caldron of boiling oil, and he is caught in his own machinations. He dies rhetorically, anticipating the hellish heats to come:

> But now begins the extremity of heat
> To pinch me with intolerable pangs.
> Die, life! Fly, soul! Tongue, curse thy fill, and die!
>   (V. v. 87–89)

The play ends with the usual homiletics: "So, march away, and let due praise be given/Neither to fate nor fortune, but to heaven" (V. v. 123–4).

Not all readers can agree that this last speech is "completely in key with the play's harsh and disenchanted mood."[13] It ends as Elizabethan plays generally end: with the meting out of justice and the pointing up of morals, relevant or not. Clearly Barabas, the Machiavellian Jew, deserves to be caught in his own trap; he belongs in the boiling caldron. To leave him free, rewarded with power and wealth, would indeed be "harsh and disenchanted"—it is the sort of thing to be found in *The Alchemist* by Ben Jonson. In any Elizabethan play we would expect to see Ferneze, the rather fatuous Christian governor, restored. In short, the play ends conventionally. For all its incidental, ironic comment on heaven, the Christians win, and the infidels lose in proportion to their malice. That the Christians have not been paragons of virtue can surprise nobody, and no one can be astonished that until the final summing up the good suffer with the bad: this is the way of the world.

We hardly know how the play might better end. The audience has had its saturnalian holiday cheering its villain, scorning the Christian hero, delighting in the reversals of stage action. And now it is time to return to the world of ordinary experience, where Christian monarchs rule, Jews are infidels until converted, and rewards and merits are often ill matched. *The Jew of Malta*, not a "terribly serious" play, is a professional piece of theater. It touches on Christian hypocrisy, hardly a new or startling theme, and its diabolical protagonist, in this fairy tale world, ultimately gets his just deserts. Essentially, this play is a comedy, in a traditional kind of way. It begins in chaos and ends in order, its disruptive elements either expelled or controlled at last. *The Jew of Malta* resembles *Tamburlaine* in its admiration of the exceptional man; *Faustus* in its deliberate exploitation of stagecraft; and its general skeptical temper is typical of Marlowe. But it is not profoundly critical like Jonson's *Volpone*, or moving like Shakespeare's *Merchant of Venice*, or cynical. Indeed, it is not of a piece; it is calculated entertainment and we must not overread it.

Just as the high themes of power and its necessary restraint are not uniformly sustained in *The Jew*—these are recurrent ideas in Marlowe's other plays—so the rhetoric of this play is also not uniform. *The Jew* has two basic styles: high flown rhetoric which recalls the triumphs of *Tamburlaine*, and plain language which anticipates the accomplishments of *Edward II*. In some speeches in this play, we find the extravagance which we have come to associate with Marlowe's name; but in others we find a new, plain, straightforward manner which has some of the virtues of prose. Barabas' opening speech is in the habitual Marlovian manner:

> Bags of fiery opals, sapphires, amethysts,
> Jacinths, hard topaz, grass-green emeralds,

> Beauteous rubies, sparkling diamonds,
> And seld-seen costly stones of so great price
> As one of them, indifferently rated
> And of a carat of this quantity,
> May serve in peril of calamity
> To ransom great kings from captivity—
> This is the ware wherein consists my wealth.
> (I. i. 25–33)

In such speeches as this Marlowe tries to "enclose/Infinite riches in a little room" (I. i. 36–37). Barabas often speaks in this high style with its vagueness and richness, but others also use it— Bosco and Ferneze (II.ii), Ithamore (II.iii; IV. iv), Calymath (V.iii), and others. The ornate rhetoric occurs most frequently but by no means exclusively in the early parts of the play.

In contrast to the high colors of the ornate style, there is a second, low style in *The Jew of Malta*. Its speeches and sentences are shorter, its imagery more earthbound, its references more exact, its diction more nearly that of ordinary speech. Ferneze and the Turks discuss their affairs in it (I.ii), and Barabas uses it in talking to Mathias (II. iii) and in plotting with Ferneze (V.ii). This plain style, which sometimes becomes prose, is most appropriate to dialogue in which there is a quick exchange between two or more persons. With such language Barabas evades the questioning of the Friars (II.i), Pilia-Borza orders Ithamore about (IV. iv), and, perhaps most effective of all, Barabas talks to an accuser (I. ii)—the parenthesis marks are added here to point up the dramatic nature of his speech:

> Blind, friar? I reck not thy persuasions—
> (The board is markèd thus that covers it—[*Aside to her.*])
> For I had rather die than see her thus.
> Wilt thou forsake me too in my distress,
> Seducèd daughter? (Go, forget not. *Aside to her.*)
> Becomes it Jews to be so credulous?
> (Tomorrow early I'll be at the door. *Aside to her.*)
> No, come not at me. If thou wilt be damned,
> Forget me, see me not, and so be gone.
> Farewell; (remember tomorrow morning. *Aside* [*to her*].)
> Out, out, thou wretch! (I. ii. 353–63)

These lines suggest the rhythms and patterns of ordinary language. Their style, which approximates the colloquial, is something new in Marlowe's drama.

In *Tamburlaine* and in *Doctor Faustus* there is very little dialogue, for they are so dominated by their protagonists as almost to be monodramas. *The Jew of Malta* differs from these plays in that here there is real interplay among the dramatis personae. The plain style of this play reflects Marlowe's new concern for human conflict in action. In *The Jew* rhetoric continues to function dramatically, in its own right, as a surrogate for action—this is the method of *Tamburlaine*—but rhetoric is also, sometimes, subordinated to the dramatic movement. In *Edward II*, Marlowe's last play, rhetoric submits consistently to the requirements of the complex dramatic moment. *The Jew of Malta* is, therefore, a transitional play, one looking backward to the high style and forward to the functional middle style, but it is no more consistent in its rhetoric than in its dramaturgy. This is a play of moments, a hasty but skillful scenario for the theater, written by a craftsman who is learning a new theatrical language.

III The Massacre at Paris

The single text of *The Massacre at Paris* which has survived was printed much earlier than the surviving text of *The Jew of Malta*, but it is in even sorrier shape. It appeared in a badly garbled quarto in 1594, and it runs to only 1,250 lines compared to *The Jew's* 2,400 lines, a more nearly normal length. Although our version of *The Jew* appears to have been corrupted by seventeenth-century editing, no one doubts that Marlowe alone wrote all of what we have of *The Massacre*. Even though the full work is hardly more than a précis of a play, every scene contains evidence of his manner. First produced by Henslowe in January, 1593, some months before Marlowe's sensational death in May, it may have been Marlowe's last dramatic work. Like *The Jew* it was successful on the stage, perhaps because it dealt with contemporary history; but it has not received much attention since. This neglect is to be regretted; for, as Boas states, the play "has a more important place in the canon of [Marlowe's] works" than has always been allowed.[14] An examination of it might well illuminate Marlowe's total achievement.

Theatricalism

Coming to *The Massacre at Paris* from *The Jew of Malta*—or from any other play by Marlowe—we are first struck by its temper. Where *Tamburlaine* and *The Jew* are notably insouciant, in spite of their fire and blood, *The Massacre* is singularly without gaiety. Death's-head jesting appears often enough in all Marlowe's plays, but here the jokes raise no laugh. The historical incident out of which the play is made is certainly harsh: the bloody attempt of the Duke of Guise and his Catholic party to put down the Huguenots in France. On St. Bartholomew's Day, August 24, 1572, Guise and his followers, supported by Catherine de Medici and her son King Charles IX, fell on the Protestants of Paris and murdered some thirty thousand of them in the streets. Marlowe's lurid play deals with the preparations for the massacre and its political consequences; the heart of the play dramatizes the killing itself—in quick succession nearly twenty persons meet violent death on the stage before our eyes. *The Massacre* is thus Marlovian in its Machiavellian concern for power and its bloodshed, if not in its grimness.

Each of the staged violent deaths is accompanied with a play of wit which is not funny. When Guise falls upon Loreine, a Protestant preacher, he kills him with a parody of liturgical ritual (vi); when Mountsorrel murders Seroune, he makes a joke about the intercession of the saints (vii); when Ramus the logician is struck down, he falls arguing with his murderer (viii); and when the schoolmasters are taken, they are appropriately "whipped to death with a poniard's point" (viii). But we cannot laugh at these scenes; they are too sinister, too unqualified. The play contains yet other grisly jokes. In one scene, for example, when a cutpurse steals his gold buttons, Mugeroun cuts off his ear in full view of the audience (xiii).

The Massacre at Paris has a sadistic temper, and its comic turns are heightened by sadism. In the other plays, and very notably in *Tamburlaine*, Marlowe carefully shields us from the full force of bloody violence by the arrangement of scenes, by the formality of language, and by the shrewd placement of sympathetic and unsympathetic characters. The brilliance of his dramaturgy is expended to force our reactions against our judgments. But in *The Massacre* the violence is candidly brought forward, and we are repulsed. The wit only heightens our revulsion. We wonder if and how the full body of the play might have modified the bloody horror of these spectacles.[15]

Although the general temper of the play is different from *Tamburlaine* and *The Jew of Malta*, the planning of the stage action from beginning to end is just as professional. Each scene is carefully calculated for maximum dramatic effectiveness. The play divides itself into four dramatic episodes. The first—scenes i through iv—is expository. It begins with a seeming reconciliation between the contending French parties. From the start any blame for future disruptions seems to rest with Guise and the Queen-Mother. In the second scene—this one has probably been cut less than any other in the play—Guise is fully characterized. We see him with an apothecary from whom he buys poison; and then we see him with a soldier, from whom he commissions a murder. He is clever, as exemplified by his use of poisons, and strong, as exemplified by his use of arms. There follows his celebrated confession:

> . . . peril is the chiefest way to happiness,
> And resolution honor's fairest aim.
> What glory is there in a common good
> That hangs for every peasant to achieve?
> That like I best that flies beyond my reach.
> Set me to scale the high pyramidès
> And thereon set the diadem of France;
> I'll either rend it with my nails to naught
> Or mount the top with my aspiring wings,
> Although my downfall be the deepest hell.
>   (ii. 38–47)

These aspirations are of a different sort from Tamburlaine's or Faustus'. As Una Ellis-Fermor has observed, "In the Duke of Guise there is nothing undefined; his desire is precise, limited and obtainable."[16] But he is no opportunist; he calculates far in advance of the event, and he is not moved by circumstance. Nor is he irrational in his aspiration, and his restlessness is not absolute. He does not reach beyond human possibility and has no need for Mephistophilis. He wants the throne of France, and he sees himself as Caesar (ii. 100); but this Caesarism is human, not divine. The world offers room enough for *him* to bustle in.

Theatricalism

If the full play were up to the quality of this speech just quoted, *The Massacre at Paris* would take its place with Marlowe's greatest achievements. After this long rhetorical scene (ii) Marlowe provides two excessively short scenes of swift action. They are complementary, for the first shows us the court of Navarre attacked by the poison supplied by Guise's apothecary; the second, the court of Charles corrupted by Guise's violent plotting. The conflicting parties, each with its leader and its spirit, are now before us; and the action may proceed. We feel sure that if these scenes were developed with Marlovian verse they would have been dramatically impressive.

The second section of the play consists of the next six scenes —v through xi. They are episodes of massacre, and their relationship to one another is careful. Before a series of vignettes of bloody violence—the murder on stage of defenseless ministers, scholars, and laymen—the Lord High Admiral is stabbed in his bed, his body thrown down, his head and hands cut off "for a present to the Pope" (v. 44). The violence thus begins with a Protestant attack against a Catholic. The shortness of the subsequent bloody scenes suggests something of the confusion of general movement. The scene with Ramus (viii) is particularly important in this series, because it provides not only the "intellectual counterpart of the physical struggle going on outside Ramus' house,"[17] but because it allows us to see that Guise, like Faustus, is at home in intellectual as well as martial worlds. Guise is no ordinary Nazi; he is a Renaissance villain. Nor is the scene between Anjou and the Lords of Poland extraneous (ix)—Anjou accepts the election to the Polish throne on the condition that he can return to France should he succeed to that throne. This scene is apparently intended to suggest that the ambitions which characterize the Duke of Guise are not confined to France—that the Machiavellian disease is general.

In the third group of scenes—xii through xviii—we are in the French court and discover its essential corruption. When Charles IX recognizes his guilt in the Bartholomew Massacre and dies, he is replaced by Henry III, recalled from Poland (xii). The new king, like the English Edward II, devotes himself to his minions: "Think they Henry's heart/ Will not both harbor love and majesty?" he asks (xiii. 16–17). The persons of his court are, if anything, worse than he. Catherine de Medici, whom we have already seen as a kind of female Guise (x. 38–46), has a genuine devotion to a religion that her male counterpart would use for his own purposes. Now she shows herself, like Tamburlaine and Barabas, to be capable of "dispatching" her own child (xiii. 61–69). Next we see that the Duchess of Guise is unfaithful to her husband, and at last (xviii) we see King Henry setting out to double-cross Guise as his predecessor had double-crossed the Admiral (iv). By fishing in these troubled waters Guise expects to mount the French throne. He fights on two fronts. First he tries to dispatch the Protestants, by massacre; then he attempts to overpower the King himself. Like Mortimer Junior in *Edward II*, this ambitious usurper rises high on Fortune's wheel.

Significantly, his chief opponents are not more attractive than he is. The King is weak, double faced, and frivolous; and Navarre, his antagonist and the leader of the Huguenots, seems cut of Guise's cloth. Navarre explains his own motives:

> The power of vengeance now encamps itself
> Upon the haughty mountains of my breast,
> Plays with her gory colors of revenge,
> Whom I respect as leaves of boasting green,
> That change their color when the winter comes,
> When I shall vaunt as victor in revenge.   (xv. 20–25)

These words are strikingly inconsistent with Navarre's habitual piety: "But God, we know, will always put them down/That lift themselves against the perfect truth . . ." (xvii. 12–13).

Navarre's protestations of Christian faith, like Ferneze's in *The Jew of Malta*, seem superficial. They may be cant, but we cannot be sure how Marlowe intends us to take them. If they are hypocritical, they are not simply so. Navarre is a Protestant and too consistently associated with Queen Elizabeth of England, in whose praise Marlowe is unambiguous, to be a simple hypocrite. (We can only wonder how Marlowe would have reacted to Navarre's subsequent conversion to Catholicism, saying "Paris is worth a mass.") As Navarre is presented here, he seems to act from one set of motives—ambition and revenge—while believing himself to be acting from another. But the text is so abbreviated we cannot be sure what Marlowe may have intended us to understand.

The final section of the play—scenes xix through xxiii—brings us to the downfall of the Guise and Henry III and to the accession of Navarre to the throne as Henry IV; and these scenes are hardly less bloody than those we have already witnessed. At the very moment the Guise thinks himself to "triumph o'er this wanton king" (xx. 53), he is struck down in the King's chambers by hired murderers. He goes to his death, though warned of imminent danger, asserting his identity with Caesar; and he, like Barabas, goes unrepentant, defiant, execrating his enemies. Unlike Tamburlaine and even Barabas, the Guise inspires no ambiguous sympathy; for Marlowe has carefully mustered all possible elements of disparagement in his death speech. In a succeeding short scene, Guise's brother, the Cardinal, is strangled, presumably killed in this manner so that the murderer's hands will not be defiled with a churchman's blood. The Duke Dumaine, Guise's other brother, now plots with a friar to murder Henry III. In the last scene of the play the King is stabbed and, dying, calls on England to avenge his popish death. The play ends with Navarre, now king, swearing vengeance on Rome and "all those popish prelates there" (xxiii. 107).

The pattern of action in *The Massacre at Paris* is sophisticated. We can see what Marlowe had in mind, and we can see his dramaturgical skill. The play pretty clearly set out to show religious and political order rising from insurgent chaos. The plan was somewhat upset because Marlowe or his abridger became fascinated with a villain who possessed extraordinary power; but we wonder if the condemnation of the Guise would be so unqualified if we had all the play.

As it stands, *The Massacre at Paris*, like *The Jew of Malta*, is transitional. It contains a number of Marlowe's standard subjects —the hypocrisy of churchmen, violence, blood, Caesarism—all so prominent in the earliest plays. But *The Massacre* also looks forward to *Edward II*, Marlowe's other history play. Both deal with historical personages and events; in both Marlowe deserts the legendary world of Faustus, Tamburlaine, and Aeneas for a world of political reality; in both a powerful and revolutionary noble overcomes a wanton king only to be deposed himself; and both contain ambitious queens. Unfortunately, abbreviation makes all of this unsubtle in *The Massacre at Paris*.

CHAPTER 6

The Unity of Edward II

I *The Problems of* Edward II

THE TROUBLESOME *Reign and Lamentable Death of Edward the Second* is Marlowe's most mature play architectonically. In it the "mighty line" is subordinated to dramatic exigencies; and the characterizations, though not so full as in Shakespeare's *Richard II*, are more nearly in his manner. The single pageant of heroic action, which we see in Marlowe's early plays, is replaced in *Edward II* by a relatively complex interaction among a variety of dramatis personae. Like other well-made plays, the action is orderly; but ultimately it is perhaps a little thin.

Apparently written in 1592 and produced in London that winter, the play was entered in the Stationers' Register on July 6, 1593, only five weeks after Marlowe's violent death, and printed the next year. The play survives in four editions, which were successively copied from one another. The basic text is the best available for any of Marlowe's plays with the possible exception of *Tamburlaine*. Since his other plays are preserved in such miserable disorder, this excellence is worthy of note and perhaps of speculation. *Edward II* in its own time was reasonably popular; and in the next generation it was revived at least twice. Never

The Unity of *Edward II*

without its admirers—Charles Lamb said that "the death-scene of Marlowe's king moves pity and terror beyond any scene ancient or modern with which I am acquainted"—it has been only infrequently played professionally.[1] College students both here and abroad have occasionally produced it, but that is about all.[2]

The neglect of *Edward II* is due primarily to its homosexuality. Until very recently homosexuality was rarely treated on the English stage, and Marlowe's treatment may have seemed especially offensive. Marlowe coolly accepts it as part of his dramatic situation, without apology or even explanation, as a simple matter of fact. The chief emphasis in *Edward II* is on civil authority, and the King's sexual eccentricity is always subordinated to that. If we neither exaggerate nor muffle the perversion, "from whatever kindly intention," as William Empson says, this aspect need not keep us from the considerable pleasure the drama offers.[3]

Coming to Marlowe's play from Shakespeare, we quickly note that, although Marlowe's play deals with historical events, his is no exposition of standard Tudor historical opinion. Marlowe's philosophical assumptions are sharply different from Shakespeare's.[4] According to Shakespeare and the Tudor historians, the events of the past illustrate the workings of divine providence. Through a study of history, it was thought, God's divine plan could be determined. Marlowe apparently did not share this Christian view of history—at least *Edward II* makes no use of it. At no time do the King and Mortimer see the ethical pattern in historical events which Shakespeare's historical protagonists so regularly discover, nor do they conceive of themselves as fulfilling a holy destiny. There is no supernatural power in Marlowe's world or in its history. For Marlowe, triumph and destruction come from a combination of human activity and accident—nothing more.

The god-less nature of Marlowe's world links this play most firmly to his Machiavellian plays, *The Jew of Malta* and *The Massacre at Paris*. *Edward II* is also a Machiavellian play, not because it contains an ambitious figure who will halt at no violence to achieve his ambitions, but because Marlowe makes a total distinction between moral and political action. Ambitious men—the Mortimers and Edwards of the world—are restrained only by power greater than their own, not by ethical considerations or by divine intervention. When Professor Ribner suggests that a lack of public virtue destroys Edward and that a lack of private virtue destroys Mortimer, he means that both conceive of self-interest too narrowly.[5] They are not sufficiently prudential, and in Marlowe's world, as in Machiavelli's, prudence is the terminal value. In neither is there an absolute law or a just God.

Edward II is notable, therefore, among Elizabethan plays, first, because of its bland use of then forbidden subject matter and, second, because of its equally bland unreligious, even irreligious, assumptions. Hints of both are to be found in Marlowe's other works—the homosexual theme appears in *Dido* and in *Hero and Leander* and the anti-theological bias in *The Jew, Tamburlaine,* and even in *Doctor Faustus.* In *Edward II,* however, these matters are not debated; for the sharp issues of this play lie in the relationship of the characters to one another, not in the conflict of ideas. Unlike *Tamburlaine* and *Faustus,* Marlowe's other great plays, this one is a tragedy of character before it is a drama of philosophical speculation.

Some critics have thought that its scenes follow so quickly upon one another as not to allow for the development of character or of "emotional significance of particular moments."[6] The play does contain a good number of scenes, some exceedingly short, and, when read, may seem episodic. Seen or imagined in the theater, however, this would not be so; on stage, the actions move swiftly but smoothly from one to the next without intermission. It is worth noting that the original text had neither act nor scene divisions. "The structural unity of *Edward II* is neither the act nor the scene, but what may be called the scenic section," one critic has correctly observed.[7] If we do not impose the conventional five-act structure on the play but attempt to define its "scenic sections," we may discover how its developing material is arranged around developing themes. We may then appreciate its excellences.

II *The First Part of* Edward II

Edward II is divided logically into three sections. The first, which for clarity's sake might be called "The King's Minion,"

extends from the beginning of the play through Act II, scene iii.
At this point Kent, the King's brother, is rejected and joins Mortimer's company of rebelling nobles. The second section of the
play, which might be called "The King's War," extends to Act
IV, scene iii. By this point the King seems to have defeated the
rebels, but we know that they are gathering strength to attack
once more. The third and final section of the play could be
called "The King's Death." At the end of the play not only has
the King been deposed and murdered, but the chief of the rebels
has also fallen. The country is finally in the hands of the legitimate heir, Edward III; and the drama ends in esthetic repose.
This is the story of a king rather than of a kingdom, of a man's
life rather than an epoch. All the action follows inevitably from
an initial human situation, and its historicity is only incidental.

The atmosphere of the first part of the play is luxurious and
Italianate. Gaveston, the King's minion, sets the tone in speeches
which recall the elaborate style of Marlowe's earlier work. When
the King writes: "Come, Gaveston,/And share the kingdom with
thy dearest friend" (I.i. 1–2), the kingdom to which he refers
is one of pleasure. In the first two soliloquies, we learn that the
King's minion will delight himself and his monarch with Italian
masques by night, with sweet speeches, comedies, and pleasing
shows:

> And in the day, when he shall walk abroad,
> Like sylvan nymphs my pages shall be clad,
> My men, like satyrs grazing on the lawns,
> Shall with their goat-feet dance an antic hay.
> Sometime a lovely boy in Dian's shape,
> With hair that gilds the water as it glides,
> Crownets of pearl about his naked arms,
> And in his sportful hands an olive tree,
> To hide those parts which men delight to see,
> Shall bathe him in a spring. . . .   (I.i. 57–66)

Gaveston's luxurious nature is defined in action as well as in
words. In a little emblematic episode, he rejects three poor men
who sue for his support (I.i. 25–50); and, by the time he meets
the King, we understand that he, like the King, subordinates
general welfare to private delights. Gaveston has an almost feminine passivity; he does not seek out the King but allows the

King to seek him. Like any courtesan, he sees it as his business to inspire love, not necessarily to love; and his attachment to the King is not separable from his desire to gratify his cultivated appetites. He bothers to make himself attractive to nobody, except the one to whom he directs his calculated charm; and that we and the court alike find him repulsive is quite irrelevant.

From the beginning of the play, it is clear that Marlowe's sense of theater is as notable as his understanding of courtesan psychology. By showing Edward as the aggressor in this relationship, Marlowe places the responsibility on him and centers his play firmly on the King. Shortly we see Gaveston and the Queen with the King (I.iv. 144–67); and, by bringing all three on stage at once, Marlowe dramatizes the King's instability.

Gaveston's supercilious wittiness throughout this first section of the play contrasts with the straightforward anger of the English barons. But it has not been sufficiently observed that, from the very beginning, these nobles are subtly differentiated. Lancaster, whom we meet first, is a temperate man seeking a logical course of action. He tries to reason with the King, and he tries to rationalize his own course. An English conservative, he is continually amazed at both the King and his own rebellion. Empires have been built on such men.

Lancaster's masculine restraint contrasts with young Mortimer's impetuosity. Young Mortimer is the leader of the rebel barons; and, when we first meet him, he defends his honor vigorously. Not rational, like Lancaster, or ruthless, like Warwick, he seems an uncomplicated soldier, one little experienced in the Italianate deviousness of Edward's court. In his English way, Mortimer is offended that the King should prefer "that base peasant," Gaveston, (I.iv. 7) to the established aristocracy. Shakespeare's Bolingbroke in *Richard II* is a good deal like him; both at first want only their legal rights, those rights which the King has clearly usurped, and their case against the King is strong. Mortimer and his colleagues have cause for alarm, as we see from dramatized action; for no one is safe from the King's caprice.

The impetuosity of Mortimer Junior is sharply contrasted to Kent's settled reasonableness. Kent, the King's brother, is the voice of legitimacy advising the King with the authority of tradition; and his judgments guide ours. Rather symbolic, more choric than individual, Kent is one of a number of analogous figures in Tudor and Elizabethan drama. Richard II is advised by Gaunt as Kent advises Edward; King Johan and Respublica, the morality monarchs in the antique morality plays of those names, have advisers of the same sort. Antony has Enobarbus, and King Lear has another Kent. Marlowe's Kent is, however, less complicated than Shakespeare's advisers; and he is more interesting than the morality figures from which such characters descend.

The two major figures in the first section of *Edward II* deserve careful scrutiny, for the characterization of the King has often been misunderstood. Even weaker than Richard II, in the early part of the play Edward is very young, newly come to manhood as well as to the throne. Though he foolishly flaunts the will of the nobles concerning Gaveston, he does not resist their usurpation of his royal dignity: he does not protect his crown so much as he attempts to defend his private rights. For Edward, the monarchy is a possession; and he has no sense of responsibility for the welfare of the realm. The barons, including Mortimer, are also not concerned with the general welfare—indeed a concern for it never appears in this play, nor does the idea of England as an entity. Edward and his nobles all want their "cut," that is all; and, when the play begins, Edward is withholding the nobles' share. This play contains nothing comparable to Gaunt's famous apostrophe to the spirit of the land—"This blessed plot, this earth, this realm, this England" (II.i. 50)—to raise the civil issue above private strife over private property. The conflict in *Edward II* is a squabble over property rights.

However imprudent, the King, like Shakespeare's Richard II, shrewdly judges the nature of the persons about him. From the beginning, Edward is aware that Mortimer reaches for more authority than his birth allows. What Edward sees more quickly than Mortimer himself is the path which the rebel must follow. The King knows that the Queen and Mortimer will ally themselves against him (I.iv. 144ff), and he recognizes the alliance the moment it is formed (I.iv. 320). The Queen, in this early part of the play, is much neglected by Edward; but there is an element of coquetry in her earliest relationship to Mortimer, and, when she is finally and completely rejected by the King, she turns to him with almost startling rapidity. This swift change is not an inconsistency in her character, for Queen Isabella is the kind of woman who feels her way to conclusions. She does not think, and Edward knows it. She is herself surprised at her conduct; but, from the start, she has prepared for her life away from Edward and in alliance with Mortimer. In her subsequent liaison, she is subtle, clever in deception, and shrewd in hypocrisy.

Marlowe is here trying to dramatize a truth of human nature, for he "knew that a woman's frustrated love could turn rancid" as Clifford Leech has said.[8] He wants to show her in the very process of development (I. iv. 170–86), but he does not have the technical proficiency to accomplish this feat. He is unable to give Isabella language which fully exploits the psychological complexity of her situation. Even so, he has written a part for acting; he has provided the raw material out of which a magnificent stage personage could be constructed by a competent actress.

In this first section of the play, "The King's Minion," our sympathies rest with the rebellious barons more than with King Edward. We prefer Mortimer's party to the King's because it is the less unattractive, not because it represents any absolute virtue. Mortimer is strong, and a state needs a strong head; Edward is willful even before his affair with Gaveston shows him to be concupiscent. This willfulness is exhibited in his relationship to Baldock and young Spencer. When Gaveston is finally executed, Edward immediately turns to these new minions. By substituting one set of favorites for another, Marlowe provides dramatic variety; but he also defines his dramatic issue. Edward's passion for Gaveston is less love than self-indulgence, and he cares for his friend less than he cares for his own emotions. We are asked to be concerned with the King's fundamental character, not his favorites. This play is about Edward's state of being, not his conduct or his friends.

When staged, this first section of the play should be spectacular. All the necessary exposition is provided dramatically in the very first scene; and, beginning with the next pair of scenes, we immediately begin to see the consequences of the given situation. Queen Isabella's conventional dignity and grief are con-

trasted to Gaveston's sardonic self-assurance. We may imagine
Isabella, Lancaster, and Mortimer on one side of the great stage
(I.ii.), Gaveston insolently eavesdropping on the opposite (I.iii.).
The language that each of the two groups uses here and through-
out this section of the play is appropriate to its manner and place.
The King and Gaveston speak extravagantly:

> My heart is as an anvil unto sorrow,
> Which beats upon it like the Cyclops' hammers
> And with the noise turns up my giddy brain
> And makes me frantic for my Gaveston.
>
> (I.iv. 311–14)

Mortimer's standard speech, in contrast, is vigorous; but it hardly
comes to our attention as verse at all. Fairly stripped of imagery,
the few figures communicate vividly:

> . . . when the commons and the nobles join,
> 'Tis not the king can buckler Gaveston.
> We'll pull him from the strongest hold he hath.
>
> (I.iv. 287–89)

Perhaps even more important than the style of individual speech
is the relation of the speeches to one another. In *Tamburlaine*
the characteristic speech is an apostrophe, long and elaborate. In
Edward II the speeches are short—their average length is less
than half that of those in the earlier plays—and the characters
actually talk to one another. Occasionally they even engage in
repartee, to our delight. We have seen this less exalted, plain
style developing in *The Jew of Malta*.

In these scenes Marlowe pleases the eye as well as the ear. He
clearly indicates elaborate costuming. The King and his court
wear "a lord's revenue" on their backs: short Italian hooded
cloaks, and Tuscan caps with jewels of more value than those
in the crown. They are followed by retinues of servants in fan-
tastic liveries who strut and jest superciliously (see I.iv. 405–18).
The nobles, by contrast, are dressed soberly, perhaps in English
furs, and certainly they wear swords. Not yet in armor, they suggest the country and the fields from which they draw their
power. Spencer Junior and Baldock wear a third kind of dress:
Baldock tells us that he is "curate-like" in his plain, dark attire,
his buttons no larger than a pin (II.i. 46ff). In going to court,

he casts off the scholar's garb, replacing it with cloak and nose-gay. The first section, "The King's Minion," is a theatrical spectacle.

The episode which concludes this section of the play is notably if subtly stageworthy. Gaveston has now been returned from his second exile because of the Queen's appeal on his behalf to Mortimer; and the King has embraced him, rejecting Mortimer, Lancaster, and the others yet once more. At this point Mortimer discovers that his uncle has been taken prisoner by the Scots and that the King will not ransom him. He and Lancaster go to the King to "thunder such a peal unto his ears/ As never subject did unto his king" (II.ii. 126–27). The King appears, accompanied by Kent; but, when he sees the nobles, starts to withdraw. His exit is barred. Mortimer and Lancaster surround him, and by turn address their grievances to him. With each speech they draw closer to the silent Edward, and their dark clothing contrasts to his "garish robes"; as Lancaster towers over the young Edward, he repeats the Scots' sarcastic jig almost like a magical charm: *"Maids of England, sore may you mourn, / For your lemans you have lost at Bannocksbourn . . ."* (II.ii. 188–89).

The King is overpowered. They depart, and for a moment he has nothing to say; and then he turns angrily on Kent and banishes his faithful brother. Edward is now alone on a darkened stage. With a show of new bravado he calls for Gaveston and the court. The dark threats of the nobles are replaced by the promised splendor of Gaveston's marriage to the King's niece. The theatrical contrast is complete. The first movement of the play ends with the furtive plotting of the rebellious lords on one side of the stage (II.iii), remote from the marriage spectacle being staged behind them. Marlowe exploits the resources for which his stage was famous: language, costume, and movement.

III *The Second Part of* Edward II

The second, briefer, movement of the play, "The King's War" (II.iv–IV.iii), differs in tone from the spectacular first movement. The King and his party now appear in armor—gayer, brighter armor than the rebels, but armor nonetheless. The parties are in open contention; and, as the relationships among the characters change, so do our feelings. Until now (II.iv.) our sympathies have been with the barons more than with the King, for we have understood Edward to be wanton and incapable of justice. But Marlowe now shows us Edward's dignity in adversity, and we think him more offended against than offending, a manipulation of our feelings that has been praised by critics. The barons, who have seemed to have a just complaint against the King, now overstep their legal rights; the treacherous Warwick, violating his chivalric code, unceremoniously strikes off Gaveston's head and shocks all parties, rebel and royal alike.

The barons' party is thus blackened, and the King's party begins to gain our approval. Formerly frivolous, Gaveston gains a certain nobility in his hour of trial (II.v; III. i). He dies thinking of the King, not of himself, for, whatever their initial relationship, Gaveston finally loved Edward. Edward also inspires love in the Spencers and Baldock; although they at first attached themselves to him in hope of material reward, they remain out of fidelity to his cause. Their speech is unironical and unsarcastic, and now they become simple Englishmen. Spencer Junior's father even voluntarily joins the King, leading "a band of bowman and of pikes,/ Brown bills and targeteers" (III.ii. 36–37). The royal cause begins to have general, conservative support; and it wears a legal face. When the royal forces meet the rebels, Edward is resolute and emerges victorious from the battle. "Edward this day hath crowned him[self] king anew" (III.iii. 77).

Marlowe makes Edward's cause attractive, then, by surrounding him with admirable supporters and by modifying the evidence of his wantonness. Moreover, he underscores the illegality of the opponents. Where in the first section of the play Mortimer was a countryman defending his rights, in the middle section he exhibits burgeoning ambitions. Earlier he had allowed the Queen to persuade him to action beneficial to himself, but he did not estimate the additional advantages that would come from rebellion. Now, when the Queen approaches, he is no longer masked, from us or from himself, and he seems to be one of Marlowe's supermen:

> What, Mortimer, can raggèd stony walls
> Immure thy virtue that aspires to heaven?
> No, Edward, England's scourge, it may not be;

Mortimer's hope surmounts his fortune far.
(III.iii. 72–75)

The first section of *Edward II* dealt with the King's private relationships and their influence on public policy; this second section of the play is concerned with public action. The tone of the
two sections is established by their language. Whereas the first
section is filled with Italianate ornament, the language of the
second is simple. Even Edward's speech is now restrained. Only
the Herald, in his formal address to the King, speaks elaborately.
Renaissance brilliance is giving way to what we will shortly recognize as Gothic extravagance, and the stage is set for the final
moments of dark horror.

IV   *The Third Part of* Edward II

The first two sections of *Edward II* are quick-paced, and in
the middle section we can imagine the passing and repassing of
soldiers. In the last section, "The King's Death" (IV.iv to end),
the tempo is slowed; and in the deposition scene it becomes almost static. In this third section of the play Edward's long
Italianate speeches recall the brilliance of his court with Gaveston. Having bested his opponents, he seems at the top of Fortune's wheel. When he hears that the Queen and Mortimer,
supported by Kent and Sir John of Hainault, are leading a force
against him, he imagines himself a conquering hero and bravado
marks his cry:

> Gallop apace, bright Phoebus, through the sky,
> And dusky night, in rusty iron car,
> Between you both shorten the time, I pray,
> That I may see that most desirèd day
> When we may meet these traitors in the field.
> (IV.iii. 43–47)

The Queen, in Edward's view his chiefest traitor, defines the
nature of the barons' rebellion and underscores Edward's limitations. By putting the defining speech into the mouth of the
now unsympathetic Queen, Marlowe achieves an almost Shake-
spearean irony:

> But what's the help?
> Misgoverned kings are cause of all this wrack;
> And, Edward, thou art one among them all
> Whose looseness hath betrayed thy land to spoil
> And made the channels overflow with blood.
>
> (IV.iv. 8–12)

A battle ensues, and the King is taken. The quality of the rebel victory is shown by Mortimer's treatment of Spencer Senior. Although Spencer Senior is the oldest and worthiest of the King's party, he is executed without trial and goes faithfully to his death. With this murder, Mortimer's party is shown to be lawless.

In the next two scenes, which are arranged for their fullest dramatic effect, the King rises in dignity. He appears disguised, probably in a monk's cloak—he refers to his clothing as "feignèd weeds!" (IV.vi. 96); and, as before, the costuming is integral to the situation. His first speech is the kind that fallen Christian princes have repeated in English tragedy for generations.[9] He mouths the clichés; but he gives them new life, for his speech derives from a dramatic occasion. And Edward consciously plays the part for which he is dressed—histrionically he is the Fallen Prince. Attempting to earn the help of the Abbot, he says: "But what is he whom rule and empery/ Have not in life or death made miserable?" (IV.vi. 14–15). This speech, which invites virtuoso acting, continues: "Father, this life contemplative is heaven./ O that I might this life in quiet lead./ But we, alas, are chased. . ." (IV.vi. 20–22).

If we have any doubt that the "chase" can have any end but Edward's death, we are quickly disillusioned. Spencer Junior, who stands near, observes a "gloomy fellow in a mead below" (IV.vi. 29), a mower who bears a scythe—the grim reaper has come to cut down the King.[10] Finally separated from his friends and given into the custody of Leicester, Edward discards his monk's garb and with it his conventional piety. Stripping off his feigned weeds, he reveals kingly clothes and turns from monkly piety to royal grief, as his clothing indicates.

In the next scene (V.i.) Edward resigns his office, slowly and with the greatest pathos. Still in royal garb, his crown upon his head, he is at once the performer and the spectator. Like Richard in Shakespeare's similar scene, Edward postures. He removes his crown, holds it out to Leicester, takes it back, returns it to his head. Finally he yields it. In one last effective gesture he gives his handkerchief, wet now with his tears he says, for delivery to the Queen. His rhetorical speech is calculated for fullest stage effect. Sharply unlike other Marlowe protagonists, he admits defeat and yearns for death. From this royal rhetoric, Edward can only descend; and, when next we see him, his robes and, with them, his majesty have disappeared. Before we come to the celebrated scenes in which he is shaved in puddle water, we see Mortimer "Who now makes Fortune's wheel turn as he please" (V.ii. 53).

The remainder of *Edward II* (V.iii, iv, v, vi) is devoted to a detailed account of the King's murder. Deprived of the material splendor which he and his minions had so cherished, he is now old—"agèd," Kent says—and in rags. Standing up to the knees in channel water, starved with only sewer water to drink, his ears deafened by the sound of a continual drum, he even yet does not comprehend his part in his disaster. "O Gaveston, it is for thee that I am wronged" (V.iii. 41), he says; but he is mistaken. We are aware of his willful ignorance and of his failure to acknowledge his responsibility for his present misery. He has no self-knowledge; and, although we can pity him, we cannot respect him. Marlowe does not invite unqualified sympathy for Edward, even though, with almost sadistic delight, he spares us no details of his frightful death.

Mortimer, in contrast to Edward, is more self-knowing and even has a moment or two of genuine heroic grandeur. But he is too crass, too narrow, too limited to material ambition, to achieve tragic grandeur. Edward and he are alike in failing to measure up to their tragic possibilities. Edward as king had sought Renaissance entertainment and he called for Italianate voluptuousness; but Mortimer as Lord Protector seeks Italianate power. In his power Mortimer has lost his early Hotspur-like impetuosity and has become a Claudius; he uses his inferiors, plots remote deaths, enjoys another man's queen, and he defends his actions in the best humanistic manner. He and we see his rebellion as a private affair, as an extension of his individual aspirations, without general moral or philosophical significance. Even in the poverty of his captivity the King does not forget his courtly splendor. He remembers his royal trappings. When Lightborn, his assassin, comes to him, he sends a message to the Queen: "Tell Isabel, the queen, I looked not thus, / When for her sake I ran at tilt in France / And there unhorsed the Duke of Cleremont" (V.v. 67–69). As M. M. Mahood has observed, "Compared with the triumphs and tournaments he [has devised], life as it is has little meaning for Edward. His state of mind is one of romantic *ennui*, the feeling that life is less real than art."[11] Ironically, the King has rejected the real world so that he might live in his indulgent construction of a world. As a result, he loses both worlds. His final suffering is sharpened for us by our awareness of this former grandeur. If he were less than a king, the scene might be an Elizabethan Grand Guignol; but as it stands, coming after his fierce defense of his wanton attachment to frivolity, it is a cruelly appropriate conclusion to his life. His violent death compounds Italianate ingenuity with medieval horror lifted straight out of the chronicles of the era. Marlowe only dramatizes what the medieval historians reported, but the result is sensational theater.

This murder scene is the most spectacular of the play. It is a triumph, as Lamb knew. Varied in temper and tone, its stage effects are carefully calculated, its characterizations sure, and its language gauged to dramatic purpose. But we are repelled by it since it illustrates no broad truth and brings us to no heightened awareness of general human nature. Although the King has fallen from his high place, his fate is not the usual Elizabethan warning to the onlooker of God's providence in the affairs of men. It does not raise general speculations or provide us with a richer understanding of the eternal situation in which we must live; it shows us no hero triumphing over temptations. Instead it is an account of the death of a rather frivolous man of rather special nature under quite extraordinary circumstances. Marlowe does not generalize, and he does not allow us to do so; and as a result, the scene is ultimately and intellectually a failure.

The play does not end, however, with the death of the King. Marlowe returns us a last time to the court, where Mortimer is seen to feel a new security:

As for myself, I stand as Jove's huge tree,
And others are but shrubs compared to me.
All tremble at my name, and I fear none;
Let's see who dare impeach me for his death.
                    (V.vi. 11–14)

But King Edward III dares, although he is still a boy. He orders
Mortimer hanged and Isabella placed in the Tower. Justice is
shown to be done, and the play ends with Edward III and his
privy council calling for their funeral robes. Through this young
king, the kingdom is returned to some measure of stability. The
earlier Italianate luxury has now become Tudor sobriety. The
short capes and plumed hats of Italy are gone, and English
mourning velvet is put on. But the play ends as it began, spec-
tacularly.

At the close of *Edward II*, the King's imaginative license,
Mortimer's aspiration, Isabella's duplicity, and Gaveston's wantonness have ended in ashes. The new order is legal, we note,
not religious as we might have expected. There is a singular
lack of religious apostrophe in these final scenes, much less than
one hears in the concluding scenes of most Elizabethan tragedy.
At the end Marlowe does not take our eyes away from political
affairs. We have seen a king fall, a king who has not really understood himself or his circumstances; and we have seen a chal-
lenging rebel fall just as disastrously.

In *Doctor Faustus* Marlowe considered the farthest limits of
human aspiration; in *Tamburlaine* he took the measure of worldly
power. These plays illuminated the eternal human situation, each
in its own way. In *Edward II* the vision is narrowed: all the
dramatis personae are essentially petty and their ambitions, except for a moment now and then, are essentially confined to
material matters. It is as though Marlowe could find little in
human affairs to admire, and less to love; and he does not deeply
engage our emotions in this play. As J. B. Steane has said, "Man
is seen as a pathetic creature, bickering or suffering; and he is
still more pathetic for having been dressed in a little brief authority."[12]

Structurally, this play is the greatest of Marlowe's accomplishments, for it is the work of a thorough man of the theater. Rhe-

torically, it is also a considerable accomplishment. In *Tamburlaine* and *Doctor Faustus* Marlowe developed a style appropriate to the central idea of each play, and the speech of one character was not sharply different from that of another. In those plays Marlowe was so occupied with expressing his theme of aspiration that he did not sharply distinguish among the speakers who gave it utterance. *Edward II* is different, for there is no central overriding style within which all the characters speak. Here Edward, Gaveston, Kent, and Mortimer have their own manners; and no single figure in *Edward II* has the sustained eloquence we have marked in the other plays. But no single character needs it; the language is suited to the occasion and to the speaker.

And yet we can make some generalizations about the style of this play as opposed to the style of the other plays. Here, even in moments of high eloquence—Mortimer's valedictory, Gaveston's anticipations, Edward's abdication—the language is closer to what we have identified in *The Jew of Malta* as the plain style. Metaphors and allusions have explicit references; diction is more concrete than orotund; rhythms approximate the patterns of speech. Monologues have given place to dialogue, to real interchange among characters. Altogether, the language has been adjusted to the dramatic situation. If the rhetoric lacks some of Marlowe's earlier, glorious exuberance, it also lacks youthful excess.

But this play is more like the dramas that other Elizabethan playwrights wrote: it is a neat and orderly exposition of character and circumstance. *Doctor Faustus* and *Tamburlaine* are lyric dramas which cannot be approached at their great moments by any other writer, even by Shakespeare. They have a singular power and a sustained passion; they widen the horizons of our imaginative experience and show us unacknowledged human possibilities; but *Edward II* does not. If this is Marlowe's last play, as seems most likely, we can only conclude that the shades of dramatic conformity were closing in on him. From the evidence of this play, we can conclude that, in perfecting a dramatic form, he had constrained the Marlovian spirit. The extraordinary passions which he had earlier substituted for a sense of human brotherhood, a tolerance for weakness, and a compassion for human frailty, now seem to have deserted him. Only now and again, momentarily, does the old audacity assert itself —when for example, Mortimer says:

> Base Fortune, now I see that in thy wheel
> There is a point, to which men aspire,
> They tumble headlong down. That point I touched,
> And, seeing there was no place to mount up higher,
> Why should I grieve at my declining fall?
> Farewell, fair queen; weep not for Mortimer,
> That scorns the world, and, as a traveler,
> Goes to discover countries yet unknown.
>
> (V.vi. 59–66)

But, for the most part, *Edward II* has become as other admirable plays are: single in tone and unified in action. The glorious excesses of *Faustus* and *Tamburlaine* do not exist here; they are sacrificed to the undeniable excellences of careful plotting and single purpose. We might prefer the earlier, uneven plays, whose celebration of the spirit unafraid to voyage on strange seas of thought alone breaks ordinary dramatic modes; but we must also admire this restrained, well-made drama of character.

CHAPTER 7

The Narrator in
Hero and Leander

I *The Problems of* Hero and Leander

HERO AND LEANDER, Marlowe's unfinished narrative poem, has been popular since it was written in the early 1590's. His contemporaneous reputation rested on it more than on his plays, for these were the actors' triumphs as much as the playwright's. The earliest edition of the poem was published in 1598; but it had been entered in the Stationers' Register on September 28, 1593, four months after his death. Two 1598 editions survive, one by Marlowe's friend Edward Blount, which contained only the Marlowe poem; the other by Paul Linley, which contained not only Marlowe's fragment—now divided into two "sestiads"—but Chapman's continuation of it in four more "sestiads." Nearly a dozen editions of *Hero and Leander* appeared within the next forty years; and, as Tucker Brooke has demonstrated, there are numerous allusions to it. This Ovidian poem, generally assumed to be Marlowe's last work, was perhaps written during the time the plague forced the closing of the theaters in 1592 or 1593.

In our own time, as always, the poem has been praised; but

certain anomalies in it continue to puzzle many readers. Both Hero and Leander speak one way but act another. Hero is said to be inexperienced in the arts of love, but she behaves like a coquette. Leander is innocent, but he talks like a man of the world. It is difficult to reconcile their claimed naïveté with their sophisticated conduct. Moreover, the verse for the most part is subtle, clearly the work of a master craftsman; yet not infrequently half and double rhymes turn up which are ludicrously flat, and we drop from high romance to the colloquial. This occasional ineptness is matched by other verbal inconsistencies. Indeed, the whole poem strikes many readers as funny. Was it intended to be?

In addition to the peculiarities of character and style, the poem contains a third anomaly. Throughout it are scattered general statements of abstract truth, gnomic observations very much in the standard Elizabethan manner. The wise saws of *Hero and Leander*, however, are inappropriate to their place: indeed, they are often fatuous. We may well ask: How are we expected to react to them? Beyond this curiosity of style is another: *Hero and Leander* contains so much more myth than it needs that the mythic ornament draws attention to itself. If we assume that there are few accidents in the poem, that Marlowe knew what he was doing, then these irregularities are hard to dismiss and even harder to ignore. Altogether, we can legitimately wonder if *Hero and Leander* is lyric or satiric or tragic or one and then the other. We can legitimately inquire what principle of organization unites these apparent discrepancies.

Critics cannot agree in their judgment of the poem. Some scholars, like Tucker Brooke, see *Hero and Leander* as "one of the purest things in Elizabethan poetry. In what [Marlowe] wrote there is not an obscene word or a degenerate suggestion; everywhere he sees the marriage of true minds, the cleanliness of ocean-dewy limbs and childlike souls."[1] Douglas Bush thinks that "the poem in its total effect is an almost unclouded celebration of youthful passion and fullness of physical life."[2] Others have found the poem more complicated. Miss M. C. Bradbrook observes that it is its great "variations from one level of detachment to another that give the poem its extraordinary air of maturity and poise,"[3] and Hallett Smith accounts for some of the apparently extraneous detail by labeling it "Italianate entertainment."⁴ J. B. Steane cautions us to hear its "very great range of tones."⁵ He maintains that *Hero and Leander* dramatizes the power of fate in human affairs. Eugene B. Cantelupe, following C. S. Lewis essentially, says that "at its core lies as serious an intention and as moral a didacticism as a mythological morality by Lydgate."⁶

Most of the difficulties of *Hero and Leander* can be resolved by asking the right questions, and some of these have been raised in a perceptive recent essay by Paul M. Cubeta.⁷ We might first inquire: Who is the teller of this tale? The narrator is clearly not Christopher Marlowe; for the narrator speaks out several times in the first person. "I could tell ye," he says, "How smooth [Leander's] breast was" (I, 65–66); and he complains of his "rude pen" and his "slack muse" (I, 69, 72). He obtrudes himself on his story by saying, "Hearken a while, and I will tell you why" Cupid cannot assist Hero in her troubles (I, 385). Later the speaker says "a globe may I term this,/ By which Love sails to regions full of bliss"(II, 275–76). None of these first person references can be identified with Marlowe. The "I" is clearly the conventional poet, and all the action is reported from his single, conventional point of view.

The speaker in *Hero and Leander* can be quite fully characterized if we consider the details he chooses to include. He is no Virgil, divinely directed by the Muse to represent truth. He is not a "supernaturally inspired man who *transmits* a story received from outside himself." Although he pretends to be a "maker," he is patently a "natural man, limited to natural power," who creates his "story out of his own experience and observation."⁸ The narrator is a pedantic, humorless romantic. As we read, we are aware of the discrepancy between the inspired singer he pretends to be and the poetaster he actually is. As Professor Cubeta has written, the narrator "is a clearly discernible character with an over-active awareness of his literacy heritage and almost no ability to master it poetically" (pp. 500–501). We find very quickly that he does not perceive the implications of the dramatic situation he writes about. We understand it better than he does, and we laugh at the repeated inadvertent exposure of his claims. The pervasive humor is directed at him—it has a satiric edge.

In his satiric treatment of the poet-narrator, Marlowe writes well within an established tradition. He is imitating his great favorite, Ovid. It will be remembered that Marlowe learned his poetic craft while still at Cambridge by translating the *Amores*, some lines of which appear in *Hero and Leander*. In the *Amores*, the *Ars Amatoria*, and the *Remedia Amoris* Ovid ironically postulates a narrator of limited ability and makes sport of his lack of understanding. In two of these poems Ovid refers to Hero and Leander. As has recently been clearly shown, the tone of Ovid's poems depends on his manipulation of the role of the speaker.[9] The role of the speaker is similarly manipulated by Marlowe, who uses Ovid's story-telling technique.

II *The Poem*

We hear the voice of the conventional poet-speaker from the very first lines of *Hero and Leander*:

> On Hellespont, guilty of true love's blood,
> In view and opposite two cities stood,
> Sea-borderers, disjoin'd by Neptune's might:
> The one Abydos, the other Sestos hight.   (I, 1–4)

The first and third lines, as Steane has pointed out (p. 304), are heroic and portentous; in them, we can hear the epic singer telling a story presaging doom. Apparently at home with the Classical myth, he seems to expect us to be equally knowledgeable. The second and fourth lines, however, are almost flat-footed and matter of fact. In this beginning we alternate from the high mythic manner to the lowly factual. From the start, the speaker seems unable to sustain his elevated tone. Throughout he is repeatedly caught by what Marlowe makes a wonderful ineptness.

The story continues, factually enough: "At Sestos Hero dwelt" we are told—and then we hear how Apollo had courted her for her hair. This bit of myth is news to us who are presumed to know all about how Helle escaped from Phrixus on a ram and drowned in what is now the Hellespont. The speaker seems to have some secret information, but does not stop to tell it to us. He is unsure of his audience and uncertain what he can expect us to know.

The speaker rushes on to an account of Hero. There follows

an "excess of opulence"—to use Poirier's phrase[10]—in the narrator's account of the girl's clothing. Her white dress has green sleeves lined with purple silk and gilt stars. The outside is embroidered with scenes from myth, her skirt is blue spotted with red, and all is covered with a veil which is worked with artificial flowers and leaves. "What a strange sense of colour Hero—and the poet —show!" Poirier remarks. If we smile at this extravagance, we smile yet more broadly at the narrator's account of Hero's perfumed breath:

> Many would praise the sweet smell as she past,
> When 'twas the odour which her breath forth cast;
> And there for honey, bees have sought in vain,
> And, beat from thence, have lighted there again.
>
> (I, 21–24)

Poor Hero is burdened by her beauty, sought out as she is by honey bees that cluster about her mouth like a cloud of gnats. The picture is farcical, but the speaker does not seem to know it. Unwilling to let well enough alone, he skirts the burlesque. As Cubeta says, "The signposts of parody are everywhere" (p. 502). His sense of decorum, that central Renaissance virtue, is missing; and an ordinary sense of humor, which would have saved him, is also lacking.

The next passage tells us more about the narrator. We learn that Hero wore no gloves because her beautiful hands charmed the elements. We are reminded of Lyly's penchant for unnatural natural history, and it occurs to us that perhaps the teller is a bit old-hat, just a little out of it. By 1592 Lyly is perhaps five years behind Marlowe; and it would be like Marlowe, that glass of literary fashion, to glance at Lyly's old-fashioned mannerisms even as once in *Tamburlaine* he had glanced at his dramatic predecessors with his jab at "jigging veins of rhyming mother wits." In these passages the simplicity, even the naïveté, of the speaker—an important and prominent characteristic—is made very clear. We discover that the artificial sparrows—sparrows are traditionally symbolic of lust—perch on Hero's "buskins of shells all silvered" and then we find that once Cupid, pining for her, had

. . . imagin'd Hero was his mother;

And oftentimes into her bosom flew,
About her naked neck his bare arms threw,
And laid his childish head upon her breast,
And with still panting rock'd, there took his rest.
                                        (I, 40–44)

The speaker seems unaware of the overtones that we (and Marlowe) cannot resist. Hero's is no maternal bosom; nor, lying panting upon it, could Cupid remain a child for long! Indeed, the central irony of Hero's character is underscored in the line that follows when she is called "Venus' nun." But one devoted to Venus, the goddess of love and patroness of venery, could hardly seek to remain virginal. Indeed, "Venus' nun" is an Elizabethan euphemism for a woman of uneasy virtue. Throughout the whole opening description of Hero, the narrator's judgment of her is, therefore, much less complicated than ours. We see the descriptive details as indicative of a kind of love which seems to escape his notice. He thinks her an innocent, but she is obviously eager for love. The irony of the poem is directed at him, not at Hero or at her situation. The narrator simply misunderstands, and we smile—at him.

The ludicrous obtuseness of the speaker is made even clearer in the passage about Leander which follows. First, we observe his archaic sentence construction—"since him dwelt there none/ For whom succeeding times made great moan" (I, 53–54)—which seems harmless if rather mannered poeticizing. There follows an example of the narrator's excessive use of myth—excessive because these mythological details do not carry appropriate significance. Leander's body may be straight, but to compare it to "Circe's wand" is to remind us of its power to reduce men to beasts, hardly the implications appropriate to this moment of love's high praise. Nor can we be sure the speaker is in command of his medium when he compares the young man's neck to "delicious meat," and rhymes "tell ye" and "belly." These details are part of the speaker's general burlesquing ineptness. By the end of the first ninety lines of the poem—the general introduction—the narrator-speaker is pretty clearly characterized. He is a pretentious, rather inept, conventional mis-reader of Ovid, who, through a faulty sense of humor, offends against decorum.

The Narrator in *Hero and Leander*

We—Marlowe and the reader—smile because his theme of virtuous love and his plot are at odds.

The principal action of the story now begins. Hero visits the temple of Venus on Adonis' feast day, and we quickly see that the speaker is not only inept but obtuse. The general truths which he strives to discover in his story are absurd. He tells us tautologically, for example, that "faithful love will never turn to hate" (I, 128); then he reports that

> "It lies not in our power to love, or hate,
> For will in us is over-rul'd by fate." (I, 167–68)

This second line, as F. S. Boas has pointed out, is "the negation of the dominant spirit of Marlovian drama where the human will soars above all limitations and boasts that it holds 'the fates fast bound in iron chains.'"[11] Within the narrative context the line cannot be taken seriously, for Hero and Leander are not passive: they have sought out romantic adventure. The girl, "Vail'd to the ground, vailing her eyelids close" (I, 159), has sacrificed turtles' blood in a church decorated with the most exuberant illustrations of "heady riots, incest, rapes" (I, 144). Any maiden honestly concerned for her chastity could hardly have ventured into such a place on Adonis' feast day. Diana's temple or even Juno's would have been more appropriate.

Far from being "over-ruled by fate," Hero invites her destiny; and her prayers are answered with gratifying swiftness. "As she rose" from her oblations, she raised her eyelids and with preposterous speed: "Thence flew Love's arrow with the golden head,/ And thus Leander was enamoured" (I, 161–62). Fortunately, Hero "was strook" as quickly since "Such force and virtue hath an amorous look" (I, 166). We smile at the ironic use of *virtue* in this line and we smile at the sly innuendos which follow: "When two are stript, long ere the course begin,/ We wish that one should lose, the other win . . ." (I, 169–70). The generalizing passage (I, 167–76) ends with the most famous line of the poem: "Who ever lov'd, that lov'd not at first sight?" (I, 176). This line, we recall, was echoed by Shakespeare in *As You Like It* (III.v. 82) where it is put into the mouth of Phebe, the most self-deluded of all the pastoral characters in that play.

Since Phebe's judgment is blurred by her senses, Shakespeare guides us to the significance of Marlowe's line and, by extension, of the whole passage and of the poem. Hero and Leander are plainly sentimental; like Phebe's, their judgment and reason are blunted by a lustful will.

The narrator's funny obtuseness continues. Hardly are we told that "True love is mute" (I, 186) than Leander begins a Love oration which has a rhetorical complexity cribbed from that master of love, Ovid himself—and from others as well. As Douglas Bush observes, "he becomes the mouthpiece for the *suasoria* of a naturalistic philosopher of love."[12] Using all the standard *carpe diem* arguments, he is quite unaware that "Chaste Hero" had already said to herself, "Were I the saint he worships, I would hear him" (I, 179). Leander, we are told, is "like a bold sharp sophister" (I, 197). A *sophister* is a specious reasoner, of course; but in contemporaneous slang he was also a second- or third-year undergraduate, a sophomore.[13] The full meaning of the epithet seems lost on the narrator. This young operator has what some modern undergraduates call "a line." He is no novice at love whatever the narrator might think. The narrator reports his address at amusing length; and, when it seems about to be concluded, Hero coquettishly "did deny him so,/ As put thereby, yet might he hope for mo" (I, 311–12). Her archness with Leander—she is something of an "operator" herself!—is obscured by the speaker's generalization: "Women are won when they begin to jar" (I, 332).

Having told the eager Leander how to find his way to her dwelling, she is "tripp'd" (we are told), and "Come thither" slipped from her tongue unbidden (I, 357–58). Her color changes, but we can hardly believe that she is as startled as the narrator says; nor can we believe that she strove to resist the motions of her heart, this in spite of the narrator's tale that Cupid beat down her supplications and subjected her to love's tyranny. It is pretty clear that the narrator thinks that Hero, and, to a lesser extent Leander, are ruled by Fate, that they are pawns in a celestial game of chance. But we know that they are no such thing. They are a great deal more like Shakespeare's Troilus and Cressida than like his Romeo and Juliet. Hero and Leander cultivate their senses, extracting fullest anticipatory delights from them. They are experts at the delaying game, knowing that rhetorical and physical fencing ripens the fruit of love. Their talk of Fate, the Destinies, and Fortune is a mask for wantonness, a masque which is taken at face value by the speaker, and again we are amused.

The story of Mercury and the shepherdess, which the narrator now introduces, parallels in some respects the story of Hero and Leander. It is included to explain why their love must end tragically; but while the stories are roughly similar, the allegorical connection between them is not obvious. There is nothing at all corresponding to "Learning" in the Hero story, nor is there any mention of the poverty of scholars or the wealth of worldly men. The narrator-speaker has simply intruded himself into his poem. It has been said that Hero and Leander, like Mercury and the country maid, have rebelled against divine authority and so must suffer death;[14] but the fact is, Hero and Leander have rebelled against nothing. They have simply followed the devices and desires of their own hearts, and, of course, their love does not protect them from disaster. Altogether, the story of Mercury tells us a good deal more about the personal concerns of the speaker than about Hero and Leander.

The second sestiad, which begins at this point, continues the ironical tone already established. This is hardly surprising, for the division of the poem into sestiads was made by George Chapman. Hero continues to pretend innocence even as she coquettishly leads Leander on. If anything, she is even less sympathetically treated in this part of the poem than in the earlier. She is quite clearly the aggressor, and Leander, though said to be wonderfully inexperienced, continues his campaign. We are told that he does not understand the significance of Hero's dropped fan; and, "dallying with Hero," he suspected "Some amorous rites or other were neglected" (II, 64). But we are unpersuaded of his ignorance; on his second visit to Hero's chamber, he conducts himself with great suavity. Inspired by the occasion, as it were, he is able to "flatter, entreat, promise, protest, and swear" (II, 268); and he is successful in his assault. The second sestiad contains the usual number of tags, some fatuous, others flat, almost all funny. It contains a high proportion of ludicrous rhymes. The speaker has not become more aware of the implications of his story than he was in the first sestiad.

[135]

The second sestiad contains several episodes that deserve independent comment. Leander's first visit to Hero's turret is recounted in the same tone as his meeting with her in Venus' temple. We are sharply aware of the contrast between the lovers' asserted naïveté and their actual behavior, and we find irony everywhere. When Leander seeks to swim the Hellespont to visit Hero for a second time, he encounters Neptune, who takes him for Ganymede. The god holds the mortal under water until he nearly drowns and, after releasing him, chases him. This passage is a description of Neptune's caresses but it is also an account of how water moves against Leander, or indeed any swimmer. We smile at the implications of the scene even as we are pleased at its descriptive accuracy (II, 181–91), but the subsequent report of Hero's flight from Leander is even funnier. Jokes about girls jumping into bed, covering up their heads, and swearing that there no man can find them must have been old with Adam; but here the tale is recounted by the humorless narrator with remarkable seriousness. In this poem multiple responses are required of us at every point.

The lines that follow (II, 287ff) have been called some of "the most memorable and deeply meant couplets of the poem,"[15] but some readers find even these ironical. The speaker sees love as cruel, but Marlowe and we see its violence as necessary to its joys. As for the struggles, "In such wars," we are blandly informed, "women use but half their strength" (II, 296). The double view of the action—on the one hand, the speaker's; on the other, Marlowe's—remains to the end. *Hero and Leander* concludes with lines that have "overwhelmed the critics," as Miss Bradbrook has observed (p. 159); but they too have their double meaning. In them, the speaker lifts his eyes from the bedroom to the dawn, from Hero to Hesperus whose "day bright-bearing car" drives "ugly Night" to hell—we cannot think the young lovers have found night so ugly as the lines assert that it is. At the end, our attention is directed to Classical mythologies, and, even as the poem began, away from this particular situation. We return to the world of fable and decoration. We have never left Ovid's urbane literate society where there is an ironic disparity between experience and an account of it. Marlowe, like Ovid, has expected us to hold simultaneously differing, sometimes contradictory, views of every incident. We are delighted with the story and we are amused at the narrator's telling of it.

III   *Marlowe and the Questions of Our Time*

Hero and Leander was left unfinished by Marlowe. George Chapman implies in his continuation that he was party to Marlowe's plans for it, but his concluding sestiads are not in Marlowe's manner. They can be made to seem a logical development if, with C. S. Lewis, we give the poem a didactic reading, but most readers find Chapman's poem so different from Marlowe's that they wonder how fully Chapman understood his friend's intentions. Many speculate that Chapman appropriated a popular poem and, adding four parts of his own, forced a unity.

It is not difficult to imagine how Marlowe might have ended his story since he had pretty clearly defined his manner. Upon leaving Hero's tower, Leander would necessarily have had to swim the Hellespont yet once more. Exhausted from his sleepless night, he could hardly have resisted the advances of Neptune, who, jealous of Leander's love for Hero, could neither ignore nor forgive him. As before, Leander would be pulled to the floor of the sea; and there he would have drowned. We could not have been surprised to find Hero thereafter translated by Venus into a constellation in the heavens. Ultimately, we might have seen Hero and Leander joined yet separated, the brilliance of Hero's stars piercing to the wealthy floor of Neptune's sea where Leander lies, his bones now made pearl.

Although frequently compared to Keats's "Eve of St. Agnes," the two poems are essentially dissimilar. Where Keats strives always to bring his action close to his readers, to make them feel with Madeleine in her chamber, Marlowe does no such thing. The myth and the Italianate decoration give his story a certain esthetic distance. For Keats, physical sensation overcomes judgment; for Marlowe, irony introduces criticism. We observe the sensual experience; we do not participate in it. Keats addresses the man of feeling; Marlowe, the man of wit. Keats takes his lovers, their situation, and himself very seriously, perhaps more seriously than the lovers and their situation deserve. Marlowe thinks his characters and their situation worth noting, hardly more. His is an unpretentious poem containing no huge cloudy symbols of high romance. As Russell Fraser has said, wit, not passion, is the strength of Marlowe's poem,[16] and this astringency salvages *Hero and Leander* from the mawkish. We see each scene through two sets of eyes at once—one, those of a sympathetic romantic, the narrator; the other, the eyes of a man of experience, Marlowe himself. In the discrepancy is the delight.

Hero and Leander, which is no doubt Marlowe's last work, contains many of the defining characteristics of his manner. As usual Marlowe disparages the dignity of the gods; when they seem to take part in man's affairs, they are capricious. For the most part, human action is determined by human beings: Tamburlaine, Barabas, Doctor Faustus, and Leander are what they are by force of their own natures; and their ambitions drive them on. Their achievements are outside the law: Leander's love is illicit—just as Faustus' aspirations, Tamburlaine's ambitions, and Barabas' avarice are beyond religious and social limitations. Their rewards are worldly—power and physical delight—and they earn some measure of our admiration. Although Tamburlaine, Faustus, Barabas, and Mortimer all come to ultimate defeat, we respect their heroic attacks on orthodoxy. In a perfect universe they would not be outlaws, and their marvelous energies would have a place and a greater claim on our respect; even in this imperfect world, ordinary judgments of them seem inadequate.

Marlowe has a major place in the history of English literature. He was not deluded when he announced in the Prologue to *Tamburlaine* that with him Elizabethan drama deserted the "jigging veins of rhyming mother wits" and came to fluency. He did, in fact, discover the meter—blank verse—that is the glory of English poetry; and "Marlowe's mighty line"—the phrase is Ben Jonson's—makes him one of the makers of English literature. He was, however, more than a supremely gifted lyric poet; he was a dramatist of overwhelming originality, too. All who came after him learned through his work how to exploit the stage for intellectual, esthetic, and dramatic purposes; for he had discovered the secret of dramatic action. *Tamburlaine, Doctor Faustus,* and *Edward II* combined intellectual significance and expressive spectacle. He showed two generations and more how plays could be written and was, thus, an important technical innovator.

Marlowe was, moreover, spokesman for an influential view of life. In his work the Elizabethan spirit, the spirit of the Renaissance, is given its fullest, least ambiguous statement. In it we see the spiritual aspiration, the worldly ambitions, and the human pride which, for better or worse, have shaped the modern world. In his plays and poems we see clearly that life is to be lived, not preached over; and that the world, without apology, is its own excuse for being. Orthodoxy nowhere earns his admiration, for, like George Orwell, he hated all stinking little orthodoxies—and all orthodoxies *ipso facto* seemed little to him. They attempted to limit life itself, and life neither could nor should be restrained. The Church, the State, the family, had no hold on his allegiance. Marlowe was not a man of faith; he turned his iconoclastic eye on the values that other men held precious, and he found them unsatisfying.

He was, in fact, haunted by what are essentially philosophical questions: for what purpose were we created and for what end do we live? He asked the hard questions, and he did not oversimplify the answers. Marlowe, like us, lived in a world in which new learning put all in doubt; as John Donne wrote in "The First Anniversary":

> 'Tis all in pieces, all coherence gone,
> All just supply, and all relation;
> Prince, subject, father, son, are things forgot,
> For every man alone thinks he hath got
> To be a phoenix, and that then can be
> None of that kind of which he is, but he.
> This is the world's condition now. . . .
> (213–19)

But it is a mistake to approach Marlowe exclusively, or even primarily, as an intellectual. His plays and his poems are passionate statements of certain attitudes. They are not arguments, however, and as we read one of his plays, we participate in a dramatic experience. Examined in the light of day, many of his attitudes strike us as thin and even adolescent; within the playhouse, imagined or real, they communicate directly, their rhetoric overcoming our hesitations, their poetry charming all doubts, their stagecraft persuading our assent. As works of art, they have vitality and integrity—even as Marlowe himself.

[139]

Notes and References

Chapter One

1. Oswald Spengler, *The Decline of the West,* trans. Charles Francis Atkinson (New York, 1928), II, 291.

2. I borrow this phrase from Arthur Mizener, "The Tragedy of Marlowe's Doctor Faustus," *College English,* V (1943), 74.

3. Quoted in A. L. Rowse, *Christopher Marlowe, A Biography* (London, 1964), p. 4.

4. John Bakeless, *The Tragicall History of Christopher Marlowe* (Cambridge, Mass., 1942), I, 19.

5. William Urry, "Marlowe and Canterbury," *Times Literary Supplement,* February 13, 1964, p. 136.

6. Frederick S. Boas, *Christopher Marlowe, A Biographical and Critical Study* (Oxford, 1940), p. 7.

7. Ethel Seaton, "Marlowe's Light Reading" in *Elizabethan and Jacobean Studies Presented to Frank Percy Wilson* (Oxford, 1959), pp. 17–35.

8. Roger Ascham, *Toxophilus, the schole of shootinge,* "To all Gentlemen and Yeomen of England" (1545); reprinted conveniently in J. William Hebel, Hoyt H. Hudson, *et al.,* eds., *Tudor Poetry and Prose* (New York, 1953), p. 609.

9. Boas, p. 19.

10. Reprinted in Bakeless, I, 77. I have modernized spelling and punctuation of this and other documents.

11. Bakeless, I, 84; Philip Henderson, "Marlowe as a Messenger," *Times Literary Supplement,* June 12, 1953, p. 381.

12. Boas, p. 111.

13. Irving Ribner, "Greene's Attack on Marlowe; Some Light on *Alphonsus and Selimus,*" *Studies in Philology,* LII (1955), 162–71.

Notes and References

14. Mark Eccles, *Christopher Marlowe in London* (Cambridge, Mass., 1934), pp. 9–14.

15. Quoted in Rowse, p. 116.

16. Quoted in Boas, p. 243.

17. Quoted in Boas, p. 244.

18. Boas, pp. 250–52; Rowse, p. 195.

19. The facts concerning Marlowe's death were brilliantly recovered by Leslie Hotson and reported in *The Death of Christopher Marlowe* (New York, 1925).

20. Eugene M. Waith, "Marlowe and the Jades of Asia," *Studies in English Literature,* V (1965), 236.

21. Harry Levin, *The Overreacher, A Study of Christopher Marlowe* (London, 1954), p. 21.

22. See Bibliography.

Chapter Two

1. L. P. Wilkinson, *Ovid Recalled* (Cambridge, Eng., 1955), p. 47.

2. Marlowe's translation of Book I, Elegia XIII, line 43 reads: "The moon sleeps with Endymion every day." *The Merchant of Venice* (V.i. 109), reads: "Peace, ho! The moon sleeps with Endymion."

3. See Madeleine Doran, "Some Renaissance 'Ovids' " in Germaine Brée and others, *Literature and Society,* ed. Bernice Slote (Lincoln, 1964), pp. 44–62.

4. Una M. Ellis-Fermor, *Christopher Marlowe* (London, 1927), p. 11.

5. See L. C. Martin, ed., *Marlowe's Poems* (London, 1931), p. 16.

6. The epithet comes from Ben Jonson's poem, "To the memory of my beloved, The AUTHOR Mr. William Shakespeare:"

> For, if I thought my judgement were of yeeres,
>   I should commit thee [Shakespeare] surely with thy peeres,
> And tell, how farre thou didst our *Lily* out-shine,
>   Or sporting *Kid,* or *Marlowes* mighty line. (II. 27–30)

C. H. Herford, Percy and Evelyn Simpson, eds., *Ben Jonson* (Oxford, 1947), VIII, 391.

7. C. F. Tucker Brooke, ed., *The Works of Christopher Marlowe* (Oxford, 1910), p. 642. See also W. W. Greg, "The Copyright of *Hero and Leander,*" *The Library,* Fourth Series, XXIV (1944), 165–74.

8. "Lucan is fiery and passionate and remarkable for the grandeur of his general reflexions, but, to be frank, I consider that he is more suitable for imitation by the orator than by the poet." Quintilian, *The Institutio Oratoria,* X.i. 90, trans. H. E. Butler ("The Loeb Classical Library" [New York and London, 1922]), IV, 51.

9. Don Cameron Allen, "Marlowe's *Dido* and the Tradition" in *Essays on Shakespeare and Elizabethan Drama in Honor of Hardin Craig,* ed. Richard Hosley (Columbia, Mo., 1962), p. 68.

10. For a different interpretation see Clifford Leech, "Marlowe's Humor," *Ibid.,* pp. 69–81. Professor Leech wishes to draw our attention to

"the pervasively comic tone" (p. 70) in this and other works by Marlowe. But see also John P. Cutts, *"Dido, Queen of Carthage,"* *Notes and Queries*, CCIII (1958), 371–74.

11. See, for example, Thomas P. Harrison, "Shakespeare and Marlowe's *Dido, Queen of Carthage,"* *University of Texas Studies in English*, XXXV (1956), 57–63.

12. Douglas Cole, *Suffering and Evil in the Plays of Christopher Marlowe* (Princeton, 1962), p. 85.

13. See F. P. Wilson, *Marlowe and the Early Shakespeare* (Oxford, 1953) and Peter Alexander, "Shakespeare, Marlowe's Tutor," *Times Literary Supplement*, April 2, 1964, p. 280.

14. C. F. Tucker Brooke, ed., *The Tragedy of Dido, Queen of Carthage* (New York, 1930), p. 212, footnote to IV. v. 25–34.

15. See G. K. Hunter, *John Lyly, The Humanist as Courtier* (Cambridge, Mass., 1962).

Chapter Three

1. E. K. Chambers in a letter to the *Times Literary Supplement*, August 28, 1930, p. 684.

2. C. F. Tucker Brooke, "The Reputation of Christopher Marlowe," *Transactions of the Connecticut Academy of Sciences*, XXV (1922), 365.

3. J. B. Steane, *Marlowe, A Critical Study* (Cambridge, 1964), p. 62.

4. Wolfgang Clemen, *English Tragedy Before Shakespeare: The Development of Dramatic Speech*, trans. T. S. Dorsch (New York, 1961), p. 113; but see also pp. 127–28.

5. G. I. Duthie, "The Dramatic Structure of Marlowe's *Tamburlaine the Great, Parts I and II,"* *English Studies*, I (1948), 126.

6. F. P. Wilson, *Marlowe and the Early Shakespeare* (Oxford, 1953), p. 30.

7. Irving Ribner, *The English History Play in the Age of Shakespeare* (Princeton, 1957), p. 64.

8. See Helen Gardner, "Milton's 'Satan' and the Theme of Damnation in Elizabethan Tragedy," *English Studies*, I (1948), 46–66. Miss Gardner discusses only *Doctor Faustus*.

9. For a Christian reading of the play see Roy W. Battenhouse, *Marlowe's "Tamburlaine," A Study in Renaissance Moral Philosophy* (Nashville, 1941, 1964) and M. M. Mahood, "Marlowe's Heroes," in *Poetry and Humanism* (London, 1950), pp. 54–86. This view is carefully and fully answered by Steane, pp. 71–77.

10. J. LeGay Brereton, "Marlowe's Dramatic Art Studied in His *Tamburlaine,"* in *Writings on Elizabethan Drama* (Melbourne, 1948), pp. 67–80: quoted at length in Leo Kirschbaum, ed., *The Plays of Christopher Marlowe* (Cleveland and New York, 1962), pp. 35–39.

11. Clemen, pp. 128–29.

12. Una M. Ellis-Fermor, ed., *Tamburlaine the Great in Two Parts* (New York, 1930), p. 162; footnote to V. ii. 97–110.

13. Duthie, p. 102.

14. Moody Prior, *The Language of Tragedy* (New York, 1947), p. 45.

15. Eugene M. Waith, *The Herculean Hero in Marlowe, Chapman, Shakespeare and Dryden* (New York and London, 1962), p. 75.

16. Waith, p. 77.

17. Lynette and Evelyn Feasey, "Marlowe and the Prophetic Dooms Part I," *Notes and Queries*, CXCV (1950), 359.

18. Levin, *The Overreacher*, p. 54.

19. Ellis-Fermor, *Tamburlaine* . . . , p. 210; footnote to II. ii. 49–52: "These fine and clear lines deserve to be compared with those on the soul in the earlier part of the play (II. vii. 18–26). The two passages, taken together, furnish the best clue to Marlowe's religious thought at the period preceding the writing of *Faustus*."

20. Clemen, pp. 122, 125–26.

21. Ellis-Fermor, *Tamburlaine* . . . , p. 254; footnote to IV. iii.

22. Douglas Cole, *Suffering and Evil in the Plays of Christopher Marlowe* (Princeton, 1962), p. 111.

Chapter Four

1. E. K. Chambers, *The Elizabethan Stage* (Oxford, 1923), III, 424.

2. David M. Bevington, *From "Mankind" to Marlowe, Growth of Structure in the Popular Drama of Tudor England* (Cambridge, Mass., 1962), p. 252.

3. Chambers, III, 422.

4. W. W. Greg, ed., *Marlowe's "Doctor Faustus" 1604–1616* (Oxford, 1950), p. 10. But see also Curt A. Zimansky, "Marlowe's *Faustus*: The Date Again," *Philosophical Quarterly*, XLI (1962), 181–87.

5. W. W. Greg, "The Damnation of Faustus," *Modern Language Review*, XLI (1946), 99; reprinted in Clifford Leech, ed., *Marlowe, A Collection of Critical Essays* (Englewood Cliffs, 1964), p. 96.

6. Greg, *Marlowe's "Doctor Faustus,"* p. 98n.

7. George Coffin Taylor, "Marlowe's 'Now'" in *Elizabethan Studies and other Essays in Honor of George F. Reynolds,* University of Colorado Studies, Series B. Studies in the Humanities, II, 4 (1945), 100.

8. Clemen, *English Tragedy* . . . , p. 148.

9. See John Russell Brown, "Marlowe and the Actors," *Tulane Drama Review,* VIII (1964), 155–73; Basil Ashmore, *"Doctor Faustus" in a special version* (London, 1948).

10. Quoted in Henry Crabb Robinson, *Diary, Reminiscences, and Correspondence* (August, 1829) Thomas Sadler, ed., (Boston, 1871), II, 107: "And he repeated his remark that it is by the laborious collection of facts that even a poetical view of nature is to be corrected and authenticated. I mentioned Marlowe's 'Faust.' He burst out into an exclamation of praise. 'How greatly is it all planned!' He had thought of translating it. He was fully aware that Shakespeare did not stand alone."

11. See G. K. Hunter, "Five-Act Structure in *Doctor Faustus," Tulane*

Drama Review, VIII (1964), 77–91. I am much indebted to this interesting essay.

12. Michel Poirier, *Christopher Marlowe* (London, 1951), p. 128.

13. Greg, *Marlowe's "Doctor Faustus,"* p. 102.

14. Leo Kirschbaum, "Marlowe's *Faustus:* A Reconsideration," *Review of English Studies,* XIX (1943), 232.

15. Levin, *The Overreacher,* p. 139: "Faustus persists in regarding his fiendish attendant as a sort of oriental slave of the lamp."

16. Francis Bacon, *The Advancement of Learning,* Bk. III, chap. iv; in Francis Bacon, *Essays, Advancement of Learning, New Atlantis, and other Pieces,* Richard Foster Jones, ed. (New York, 1937), pp. 436–39.

17. Arthur Mizener, "The Tragedy of Marlowe's *Doctor Faustus,*" *College English,* V (1943), 70–75.

18. James Smith, *"Dr. Faustus,"* Scrutiny, VIII (1939–1940), 47.

19. Eric Keown, [Review], *Punch,* XXIV (August 3, 1961), 328.

20. Greg, "The Damnation of Faustus," 106; in Leech, *Marlowe,* pp. 105–06.

21. Spengler, *The Decline of the West,* II, 289.

22. Boas, *Christopher Marlowe,* p. 216.

23. Richard B. Sewall, *The Vision of Tragedy* (New Haven, 1959), p. 66.

Chapter Five

1. Alfred Harbage, "Innocent Barabas," *Tulane Drama Review,* VIII (1964), 55.

2. T. S. Eliot, "Christopher Marlowe," *Selected Essays, 1917–1932* (New York, 1932), p. 105; reprinted in Leech, *Marlowe, A Collection of Critical Essays,* p. 16.

3. L. C. Knights, *Further Explorations* (Stanford, 1965), p. 93.

4. See chap. 4, note 10.

5. For a general consideration see G. K. Hunter, "The Theology of the *Jew of Malta,*" *Journal of the Warburg and Courtauld Institutes,* XXVII (1964), 214; Arthur Lukyn Williams, *Adversus Judaeos, A Bird's-eye View of Christian 'Apologieae' until the Renaissance* (Cambridge, Eng., 1935).

6. Wilson, *Marlowe and the Early Shakespeare,* p. 58.

7. Levin, *The Overreacher,* p. 86.

8. Levin, p. 83.

9. Kirschbaum, *The Plays of Christopher Marlowe,* p. 141: "The Jew tests his tawdry human purchase as to his capacity for villainy. He tells lies about his own criminality, but, true, they are falsehoods not too far from the truth."

10. Steane, *Marlowe, A Critical Study,* p. 187.

11. H. S. Bennett, ed., *The Jew of Malta* and *The Massacre at Paris* (London, 1931), p. 15; Wilson, pp. 63–64.

12. Kirschbaum, *The Plays of Christopher Marlowe,* p. 153: "Note how completely Marlowe is using his stage: platform, tarras, trap in the tarras, tower."

Notes and References

13. Steane, p. 194.

14. Boas, *Christopher Marlowe*, p. 153.

15. Our only text for *The Massacre at Paris* appears to be a memorial reconstruction. In addition to this printed quarto, there exists a strange manuscript of some thirty-three lines which contains the beginning of a somewhat more extended version of the abbreviated printed scene (xviii). Apparently this is a section of the original play out of which the mutilated version was cut. By a close examination we can see that the original editor in 1594 intended to preserve the bones of Marlowe's action while simplifying the characters and the implications of the action. This page is referred to as the Collier Leaf after J. Payne Collier who once owned it. See John Bakeless, *The Tragicall History of Christopher Marlowe* (Cambridge, Mass., 1942), II, 91–95. Boas reprints both MS and Octavo versions of the scene, pp. 168–71.

16. Ellis-Fermor, *Christopher Marlowe*, p. 106.

17. David Galloway, "The Ramus Scene in Marlowe's *The Massacre at Paris*," *Notes and Queries*, CXCVIII (1953), 147.

Chapter Six

1. Charles Lamb, "Specimens of English Dramatic Poets" in *The Works of Charles and Mary Lamb*, E. V. Lucas, ed. (London, 1904), IV, 24.

2. See Toby Robertson, in an interview with John Russell Brown, "Directing *Edward II*," *Tulane Drama Review*, VIII (1964), 174–83.

3. William Empson, "Two Proper Crimes," *The Nation*, CLXIII (1946), 445.

4. *Edward II* has been frequently compared to Shakespeare's *Richard II*. The two plays are closely contemporaneous, and they contain similar dramatic situations similarly treated. Until recently it had been assumed that Shakespeare learned from Marlowe, Marlowe having reached theatrical prominence before him. Professor Peter Alexander has called these assumptions into question. He has shown that the two young men influenced each other, Shakespeare affecting Marlowe as much as Marlowe Shakespeare. See *Times Literary Supplement*, April 2, 1964, p. 280.

5. Ribner, *The English History Play . . .* , p. 131.

6. Clemen, *English Tragedy . . .* , p. 155.

7. Robert Fricker, "The Dramatic Structure of *Edward II*," *English Studies*, XXXIV (1953), 214. By way of contrast see chap. 4, note 11, Hunter, "Five-Act Structure in *Doctor Faustus*."

8. Clifford Leech, "Marlowe's *Edward II*: Power and Suffering," *Critical Quarterly*, I (1959), 191. See also Bevington, *From "Mankind" to Marlowe . . .* , pp. 240–41.

9. Clemen, pp. 158–59.

10. Leech, p. 193.

11. Mahood, *Poetry and Humanism*, p. 84.

12. Steane, *Marlowe, A Critical Study*, p. 206.

Chapter Seven

1. Tucker Brooke, "The Renaissance," in *A Literary History of England,* Albert C. Baugh, ed. (New York & London, 1948), p. 514.

2. Douglas Bush, *Mythology and the Renaissance Tradition in English Poetry* (rev. ed.; New York, 1963), p. 122.

3. M. C. Bradbrook, "*Hero and Leander,*" *Scrutiny,* II (1933), 60.

4. Hallett Smith, *Elizabethan Poetry, A Study in Conventions, Meaning, and Expression* (Cambridge, Mass., 1952), p. 78.

5. Steane, *Marlowe, A Critical Study,* p. 310.

6. Eugene B. Cantelupe, "*Hero and Leander,* Marlowe's Tragicomedy of Love," *College English,* XXIV (1962–63), 296; C. S. Lewis, "*Hero and Leander*" (Warton Lecture on English Poetry), *Proceedings of the British Academy* (London, 1952), pp. 23–37. See also Rosemond Tuve, *Elizabethan and Metaphysical Imagery* (Chicago, 1947), p. 158.

7. Paul M. Cubeta, "Marlowe's Poet in *Hero and Leander,*" *College English,* XXVI (1964–65), 500–05.

8. Robert M. Durling, *The Figure of the Poet in Renaissance Epic* (Cambridge, Mass., 1965), p. 9.

9. Durling, pp. 26–31.

10. Poirier, *Christopher Marlowe,* p. 198.

11. Boas, *Christopher Marlowe,* p. 230.

12. Bush, p. 129.

13. Clifford Leech, "Venus and Her Nun: Portraits of Women in Love by Shakespeare and Marlowe," *Studies in English Literature,* V (1965), 256.

14. Paul W. Miller, "A Function of Myth in Marlowe's *Hero and Leander,*" *Studies in Philology,* L (1953), 166.

15. Steane, p. 330.

16. Russell A. Fraser, "The Art of *Hero and Leander,*" *Journal of English and Germanic Philology,* LVII (1958), p. 754.

Selected Bibliography

PRIMARY SOURCES

1. *Collected Editions*

BROOKE, C. F. TUCKER (ed.). *The Works of Christopher Marlowe.* Oxford: at the Clarendon Press, 1910. The standard, old spelling edition with informative headnotes but no glosses.

CASE, R. H. (general editor). *The Works and Life of Christopher Marlowe.* 6 vols. London: Methuen and Co., 1930–33. Full notes, glossaries and introductions.

    1. Life and *Dido, Queen of Carthage*, ed. C. F. TUCKER BROOKE.

    2. *Tamburlaine the Great in Two Parts*, ed. U. M. ELLIS-FERMOR.

    3. *The Jew of Malta* and *The Massacre at Paris*, ed. H. S. BENNETT.

    4. *Poems*, ed. L. C. MARTIN. All references to poems in this book are to this edition.

    5. *Doctor Faustus*, ed. F. S. BOAS.

    6. *Edward II*, eds. H. B. CHARLTON and R. D. WALLER, revised by F. N. LEES (1955).

KIRSCHBAUM, LEO (ed.). *The Plays of Christopher Marlowe.* Cleveland and New York: Meridian Books, 1962. An eccentric text which excludes *Dido* and *The Massacre at Paris*. Elaborate scene-by-scene analysis and plot summary. Lengthy general introduction and general glossary.

RIBNER, IRVING (ed.). *The Complete Plays of Christopher Marlowe.*

New York: Odyssey Press, 1963. The standard modern edition to which all references are made in this book. Useful notes and glossaries at foot of the page; general bibliography; full textual notes.

2. Editions of Individual Works

BRIGGS, WILLIAM D. (ed.). *Edward II*. London: David Nutt, 1914. Very full introduction, notes, and commentary.

DONNO, ELIZABETH STORY (ed.). *Hero and Leander* in *Elizabethan Minor Epics*. New York: Columbia University Press, London: Routledge & Kegan Paul, 1963. Old spelling without glossary. Contains Chapman's continuation and other Ovidian poems.

GREG, W. W. (ed.). *The Tragical History of the Life and Death of Doctor Faustus, A Conjectural Reconstruction*. Oxford: at the Clarendon Press, 1950. By comparing the two authoritative editions, the leading bibliographer of his time constructs a text upon which subsequent editions are largely dependent. No notes or glossary.

GUTHRIE, TYRONE and DONALD WOLFIT. *Tamburlaine the Great, An Acting Version*. London: William Heinemann, 1951. Combines *Part One* and *Part Two* for a single spectacle.

JUMP, JOHN D. (ed.). *Tamburlaine the Great Parts I and II*. ("Regents Renaissance Drama Series."). Lincoln: University of Nebraska Press, 1967. Careful text. Notes and glossary at foot of page.

———. (ed.). *The Tragical History of the Life and Death of Doctor Faustus*. ("The Revels Plays."). Cambridge, Mass.: Harvard University Press, 1962. Complete notes, glossary, and scholarly appendices. The text is heavily indebted to Greg.

RIBNER, IRVING (ed.). *The Tragical History of the Life and Death of Doctor Faustus*. New York, Odyssey Press, 1966. Text and notes from Ribner's *Complete Plays*, plus selections from nine critics. Available in paperback.

VAN FOSSEN, RICHARD W. (ed.). *The Jew of Malta*. ("Regents Renaissance Drama Series."). Lincoln: University of Nebraska Press, 1964. Careful text. Notes and glossary at foot of page. Appendices.

3. Bibliography and Reference

CRAWFORD, CHARLES. *The Marlowe Concordance* (*Materialien zur Kunde des Älteren englischen Dramas*). 7 parts in 3 vols. Louvain: A Uystpruyst, 1911–32.

TANNENBAUM, SAMUEL A. *Marlowe* (*A Concise Bibliography*). New York: Scholars' Facsimiles and Reprints, 1937; *Supplement* by

Selected Bibliography

SAMUEL A. and DOROTHY R. TANNENBAUM. New York: Samuel
A. Tannenbaum, [1947].

SECONDARY SOURCES

The following list of studies is arranged according to topic and work
to facilitate quick reference.

1. Biographies and General Studies

BAKELESS, JOHN. *The Tragicall History of Christopher Marlowe*. 2
vols. Cambridge, Mass.: Harvard University Press, 1942. Attempts to "bring together everything that can now be known
about Christopher Marlowe." Especially valuable for factual
matter. Full bibliography and index.

BEVINGTON, DAVID M. *From "Mankind" to Marlowe, Growth of Structure in the Popular Drama of Tudor England*. Cambridge, Mass.:
Harvard University Press, 1962. Examines the relation of morality plays to later plays, including Marlowe's; original and illumi-
nating.

BOAS, FREDERICK S. *Christopher Marlowe, A Biographical and Critical
Study*. Oxford: at the Clarendon Press, 1940, 1953. Especially
strong in factual data. Many documents reproduced in original
spelling. Addressed to scholarly audience.

BROOKE, C. F. TUCKER. "The Reputation of Christopher Marlowe,"
Transactions of the Connecticut Academy of Sciences, XXV
(1922), 347–408. Definitive work on the subject.

CLEMEN, WOLFGANG. *English Tragedy Before Shakespeare, The Development of Dramatic Speech*, trans. T. S. DORSCH. New York:
Barnes & Noble, 1961. First published in German in 1955. Traces
the history of "serious drama" before Shakespeare by studying it
in relation to the set dramatic speech. Particularly useful as it
illuminates individual passages.

COLE, DOUGLAS W. *Suffering and Evil in the Plays of Christopher
Marlowe*. Princeton: Princeton University Press, 1962. Relates
the plays to the theological matters current at Cambridge in Marlowe's time.

ECCLES, MARK. *Christopher Marlowe in London*. Cambridge, Mass.:
Harvard University Press, 1934. A biographical study containing
new information.

ELIOT, THOMAS STEARNS. "Christopher Marlowe." *Selected Essays,
1917–1932*. New York: Harcourt, Brace and Co., 1932. Most
seminal of modern studies of Marlowe.

ELLIS-FERMOR, U. M. *Christopher Marlowe*. London: Methuen and
Co., 1927. Sympathetic treatment of Marlowe's mind and art with

an attempt to "portray the personality." Sensitive critical judgments.

HENDERSON, PHILIP. *Christopher Marlowe*. London, New York, Toronto: Longmans, Green and Co., 1952. Brief critical biography addressed to the general reader.

HOTSON, LESLIE. *The Death of Christopher Marlowe*. London: The Nonesuch Press; Cambridge, Mass., Harvard University Press, 1925. In this little volume, Professor Hotson tells how he discovered the circumstances of Marlowe's death. Fascinating both for its new information and for the circumstances of discovery.

KOCHER, PAUL H. *Christopher Marlowe, A Study of His Thought, Learning, and Character*. Chapel Hill: University of North Carolina Press, 1946. Standard study which, focusing on the life more than on the individual work, places Marlowe in his intellectual milieu.

LEECH, CLIFFORD (ed.). *Marlowe, A Collection of Critical Essays*. Englewood Cliffs, N. J.: Prentice-Hall, 1964. Useful assemblage of fourteen essays by Eliot, Levin, Battenhouse, Waith, Greg, Ellis-Fermor, Brockbank, Wilson, Clemen, Bevington, Kocher, and Leech.

LEVIN, HARRY. *The Overreacher, A Study of Christopher Marlowe*. Cambridge, Mass.: Harvard, University Press, 1952. Perceptive critical explication of each work. "The concept of hyperbole" is "a unifying key."

MAHOOD, M. M. "Marlowe's Heroes." *Poetry and Humanism*. London: Jonathan Cape, 1950. "Through the course of the four great tragedies, the Marlowe hero shrinks in stature from the titanic to the puny." The essay is concerned with "the downfall of the humanist ideal."

POIRIER, MICHEL. *Christopher Marlowe*. London: Chatto and Windus, 1951. General introduction intending to "paint a psychological portrait" of the man and to "assess the aesthetic value of his writings."

RIBNER, IRVING. "Marlowe's 'Tragicke Glasse.'" *Essays on Shakespeare and Elizabethan Drama in Honor of Hardin Craig*, ed. RICHARD HOSLEY. Columbia, Mo.: University of Missouri Press, 1962. Traces Marlowe's slow arrival at tragedy as he "came to recognize the frailty and limitation of humanity."

ROWSE, A.L. *Christopher Marlowe, A Biography*. London: Macmillan & Co., 1964. Addressed to a general audience. Filled with colorful detail and controversial judgments. Very spirited.

Selected Bibliography

STEANE, J. B. *Marlowe, A Critical Study.* Cambridge, Eng.: at the University Press, 1964. "Criticism that has poetry as its centre of interest." Full consideration of each work.

Tulane Drama Review, "Marlowe Issue" (VIII [1964]). Contains essays by Levin, Harbage, Barber, Waith, G. K. Hunter, Leech, Ribner, J. R. Brown, Wickham, and others. Varied, useful, often entertaining.

WILSON, F. P. *Marlowe and the Early Shakespeare.* Oxford: at the Clarendon Press, 1953. Considered judgments carefully phrased. More sharply original than at first appears.

WRAIGHT, A. D. *In Search of Christopher Marlowe, A Pictorial Biography.* New York: Vanguard Press, 1965. Photography by VIR-GINIA F. STEARN. Full account of life and times; wonderful, relevant pictures; addressed to the general audience.

2. *Life and Times*

ALEXANDER, PETER. "Shakespeare, Marlowe's Tutor," *Times Literary Supplement,* April 2, 1964, p. 280. Suggests that Shakespeare's influence on Marlowe was greater than vice versa.

BROWN, JOHN RUSSELL. "Marlowe and the Actors," *Tulane Drama Review,* VIII (1964), 155–73. Marlowe wrote these plays for a style of acting which must be reclaimed if we are to respond as Marlowe intended.

BUSH, GEOFFREY. "A Great Reckoning in a Little Room," *Atlantic Monthly,* CXCII (December, 1953), 62–67. Vivid fictional treatment of the last day of Marlowe's life, but Marlowe is viewed as softer than some persons think likely.

KOCHER, PAUL H. "Christopher Marlowe, Individualist," *University of Toronto Quarterly,* XVII (1948), 111–20. Views Marlowe as concerned with religion but opposed to "entrenched theological system"; an "inaccessible but tortured spirit."

RIBNER, IRVING. "Marlowe and the Critics," *Tulane Drama Review,* VIII (1964), 211–24. Review of criticism of Marlowe; careful consideration of recent work.

SEATON, ETHEL. "Marlowe's Light Reading." *Elizabethan and Jacobean Studies Presented to Frank Percy Wilson.* Oxford: at the Clarendon Press, 1959. Marlowe's early uncritical reading was in the popular medieval romances, the Troy legend, and the like.

URRY, WILLIAM. "Marlowe and Canterbury," *Times Literary Supplement,* February 13, 1964, p. 136. Marlowe's family's reputation in Canterbury. Contains important new information.

WAITH, EUGENE M. "Marlowe and the Jades of Asia," *Studies in English Literature*, V (1965), 229–45. Analysis of how Marlowe balanced one view against another within individual scenes. Notes complex attitudes toward characters and actions.

3. *Ovid, Lucan, and* Dido, Queen of Carthage

ALLEN, DON CAMERON. "Marlowe's *Dido* and the Tradition." *Essays on Shakespeare and Elizabethan Drama in Honor of Hardin Craig*, ed. RICHARD HOSLEY. Columbia, Mo.: University of Missouri Press, 1962. Though probably not allegorical, the play illustrates "what the Renaissance and the Middle Ages would call perverse love."

CUTTS, JOHN P. "*Dido, Queen of Carthage*," *Notes and Queries*, CCIII (1958), 371–74. Play concerned with the passion of love; love on earth contrasted to love in heaven. "Is Marlowe's overall comment one of ironic contempt for the author of heaven . . .?"

DORAN, MADELEINE. "Some Renaissance 'Ovids.'" *Literature and Society*, ed. BERNICE SLOTE. Lincoln: University of Nebraska Press, 1964. Questions validity of "typological" readings of Elizabethan texts.

HARRISON, THOMAS P. "Shakespeare and Marlowe's *Dido, Queen of Carthage*," *University of Texas Studies in English*, XXXV (1956), 57–63. Echoes of *Dido* in *Hamlet*, *A Midsummer Night's Dream*, *Antony and Cleopatra*.

LEECH, CLIFFORD. "Marlowe's Humor." *Essays on Shakespeare and Elizabethan Drama in Honor of Hardin Craig*, ed. RICHARD HOSLEY. Columbia, Mo.: University of Missouri Press, 1962. Varieties of humor in *Dido* illustrated. Also considers *The Massacre at Paris* and *Hero and Leander*.

MARTIN, L. C. "Lucan - Marlowe - ? Chapman," *Review of English Studies*, XXIV (1948), 317–21. Though Chapman may have touched up Marlowe's translation, the similarity of his Homer to Marlowe's Lucan "may indicate no more than that Chapman had taken admiring notice of Marlowe's work."

4. Tamburlaine the Great

BATTENHOUSE, ROY W. *Marlowe's "Tamburlaine," A Study in Renaissance Moral Philosophy*. Nashville, Tenn.: Vanderbilt University Press, 1941, 1964. Presents the play as didactic, conforming to conventional morality in the tradition of the *Mirror for Magistrates*.

DUTHIE, G. I. "The Dramatic Structure of Marlowe's 'Tamburlaine the Great,' Parts I and II," *English Studies*, I (1948), 101–26. Both plays have coherent dramatic structure and are "dramas in the true sense of that word."

Selected Bibliography

FEASEY, LYNETTE and EVELINE. "Marlowe and the Homilies," *Notes and Queries*, CXCV (1950), 7–10. Does Marlowe intend an ironic mockery of the Homilies?

———. "Marlowe and the Prophetic Dooms," *Notes and Queries*, CXCV (1950), 356–9, 404–7, 419–21. Marlowe uses "apocalyptic imagery" and religious references for ironic mockery of God of Wrath.

GARDNER, HELEN L. "The Second Part of 'Tamburlaine the Great,'" *Modern Language Review*, XXXVII (1942), 18–24. Marlowe's sympathies "have changed since he wrote the first part . . . and the change of theme has, in turn, necessitated a change of structure. . . . The first part of *Tamburlaine* glorifies the human will: the second displays its inevitable limits."

LEECH, CLIFFORD. "The Structure of *Tamburlaine*," *Tulane Drama Review*, VIII (1964), 32–46. Though *Part Two* echoes its predecessor, "in the range of its effects and in the depth of its implication, the sequel has some right to be considered the greater play."

LEPAGE, PETER V. "The Search for Godhead in Marlowe's *Tamburlaine*," *College English*, XXVI (1964–65), 604–09. Life of the drama is in Tamburlaine's godlike power over life and death; play has both esthetic and psychological unity.

RIBNER, IRVING. "The Idea of History in Marlowe's *Tamburlaine*," *ELH*, XX (1954), 251–66. Marlowe draws on Classical sources for philosophy of history, not on Tudor ones. Play contains a direct denial of the role of providence in human history.

SMITH, HALLETT D. "Tamburlaine and the Renaissance." *Elizabethan Studies in Honor of George F. Reynolds*. University of Colorado Studies, Series B. Studies in the Humanities, II, 4, (1945). Tamburlaine sometimes regarded as "the representative man" of the Renaissance.

WAITH, EUGENE M. *The Herculean Hero in Marlowe, Chapman, Shakespeare and Dryden*. New York: Columbia University Press; London: Chatto & Windus, 1962. "His is the intrinsic kingliness of the hero," and "the play's dominant appeal is to the wonder aroused by vast heroic potential."

5. Doctor Faustus

BARBER, C. L. " 'The form of Faustus' fortunes good or bad," *Tulane Drama Review*, VIII (1964), 92–119. Marlowe presents "blasphemy as heroic endeavor, and the tragic ironies of such endeavor."

CAMPBELL, LILY B. "*Doctor Faustus*: A Case of Conscience," *PMLA*,

LXVII (1952), 219–39. Centers attention on the sin of despair and finds analogy in a historical case.

GARDNER, HELEN. "Milton's 'Satan' and the Theme of Damnation in Elizabethan Tragedy," *English Studies*, I (1948), 46–66. Considers *Faustus, Macbeth, The Changeling* as antecedent to Milton.

GREG, W. W. "The Damnation of Faustus," *Modern Language Review*, XLI (1946), 97–107. Interprets damnation in terms of Elizabethan beliefs about spirits.

HEILMAN, ROBERT B. "The Tragedy of Knowledge: Marlowe's Treatment of Faustus," *Quarterly Review of Literature*, II (1946), 316–32. Explication of theme and action scene by scene.

HUNTER, G. K. "Five-Act Structure in *Doctor Faustus*," *Tulane Drama Review*, VIII (1964), 77–91. Play's "inner economy . . . moving forward continuously in a single direction."

KAULA, DAVID. "Time and the Timeless in *Everyman* and *Doctor Faustus*," *College English*, XXII (1960), 9–14. "The hero's destiny hinges entirely on the question of faith, a question which does not enter into *Everyman* at all."

KIRSCHBAUM, LEO. "Marlowe's *Faustus*: A Reconsideration," *Review of English Studies*, XIX (1943), 225–41. Emphasizes the theatrical nature of play and Marlowe's attention to staged conflict.

MIZENER, ARTHUR. "The Tragedy of Marlowe's Doctor Faustus," *College English*, V (1943), 70–75. Emphasizes the theme of the play and the nature of the conflict.

ORNSTEIN, ROBERT. "The Comic Synthesis in *Doctor Faustus*," *ELH*, XXII (1955), 165–72. "The slapstick scenes which tickled groundling fancies unite with the seemingly fragmented main action to form a subtly ironic tragic design."

SEWELL, RICHARD B. "*Doctor Faustus*." *The Vision of Tragedy*. New Haven: Yale University Press, 1959. "The first to explore the tragic possibilities of the head-on clash of the Renaissance compulsions with the Hebraic-Christian tradition."

SMITH, JAMES. "Marlowe's *Dr. Faustus*," *Scrutiny*, VIII (1930), 36–55. Emphasizes Faustus' diseased will.

6. The Jew of Malta *and* The Massacre at Paris

BABB, HOWARD S. "Policy in Marlowe's *The Jew of Malta*," *ELH*, XXIV (1957), 85–97. Play is unified around a single set of issues: religious hypocrisy and governmental expedience.

CARPENTER, NAN COOKE. "Infinite Riches: A Note on Marlovian Unity," *Notes and Queries*, CXCVI (1951), 50–52. Play unified about the universal desire for money.

FLOSDORF, J. W. "The 'Odi et Amo' Theme in *The Jew of Malta*,"

Notes and Queries, CCV (1960), 10–14. "Hate provides the dominant tone of the play."

GALLOWAY, DAVID. "The Ramus Scene in Marlowe's *The Massacre at Paris*," *Notes and Queries*, CXCVIII (1953), 146–47. Maligned Ramus scene has a "definite psychological and dramatic purpose."

HARBAGE, ALFRED. "Innocent Barabas," *Tulane Drama Review*, VIII (1964), 47–58. Marlowe had "little imaginative affinity with corruption; and whereas he could *invent* a limited repertory of wicked things for Barabas to do, he could not *imagine* the appropriate things for such a doer to think."

HUNTER, G. K. "The Theology of Marlowe's *The Jew of Malta*," *Journal of the Warburg and Courtauld Institutes*, XXVII (1964), 211–40. Marlowe had a "richly complex and ambivalent attitude to Christianity." Important, learned, judicious essay.

PRAZ, MARIO. "Machiavelli and the Elizabethans," *Proceedings of the British Academy*, XIV (1928), 49–97. Classic exposition of the place of Machiavelli in Elizabethan thought.

7. Edward II

BRODWIN, LEONORA LEET. "*Edward II*: Marlowe's Culminating Treatment of Love," *ELH*, XXXI (1964), 139–55. "Marlowe, in his early plays, had identified a masculine surrender to love with effeminacy . . . it would appear that Marlowe did not consider Leander's love for a woman to be in any way different from that which Gaveston might bear for Edward."

EMPSON, WILLIAM. "Two Proper Crimes," *The Nation*, CLXIII (1946), 444–45. Faustus and Edward "die because of the two crimes for which Marlowe stood boastfully and defiantly in peril of death."

FRICKER, ROBERT. "The Dramatic Structure of *Edward II*," *English Studies*, XXXIV (1953), 204–17. Emphasizes the structural unity and economy providing the "forward urge of the action."

LEECH, CLIFFORD. "Marlowe's *Edward II*: Power and Suffering," *Critical Quarterly*, I (1959), 181–96. "In *Tamburlaine* he had already contemplated power . . . Here the suffering . . . is the major fact."

MILLS, L. J. "The Meaning of *Edward II*," *Modern Philology*, XXXII (1934), 11–31. In sixteenth-century literature "when the claims of friendship clash with those of love, friendship should be given precedence."

MORRIS, HARRY. "Marlowe's Poetry," *Tulane Drama Review*, VIII (1964), 134–54. "Restraint" of poetry in *Edward II* contrasted to earlier "rants" of Tamburlaine. Careful attention given to Mortimer's speech.

RIBNER, IRVING. *The English History Play in the Age of Shakespeare.* Princeton: Princeton University Press, 1957. Play seen as a tragedy of character, not of fate or fortune.

8. Hero and Leander

BRADBROOK, M. C. "*Hero and Leander,*" *Scrutiny,* II (1933), 59–64. Careful analysis of style and tone; concludes that Marlowe is "both ironically detached and sympathetically identified with the lovers."

BUSH, DOUGLAS. "Marlowe: *Hero and Leander.*" *Mythology and the Renaissance Tradition in English Poetry.* New York: W. W. Norton & Co., rev. ed. 1963. Analysis of the poem placing it in its Classical tradition.

CANTELUPE, EUGENE B. "*Hero and Leander,* Marlowe's Tragicomedy of Love," *College English,* XXIV (1962–63), 295–98. Sees the poem as essentially didactic, preaching against passion.

CUBETA, PAUL M. "Marlowe's Poet in *Hero and Leander,*" *College English,* XXVI (1964–65), 500–05. Sees the narrator as "clearly discernible character" and the poem as a "virtuoso performance of parodying."

FRASER, RUSSELL A. "The Art of *Hero and Leander,*" *Journal of English and Germanic Philology,* LVII (1958), 743–54. The poem anti-romantic and witty, giving evidence of Marlowe's self-conscious craftsmanship.

GORDON, D. J. "Chapman's *Hero and Leander,*" *English Miscellany,* V (1954), 41–94. Warns against too simple a definition of Renaissance "kinds" including the "Ovidian" poem.

LEECH, CLIFFORD. "Venus and Her Nun: Portraits of Women in Love by Shakespeare and Marlowe," *Studies in English Literature,* V (1965), 247–68. Emphasizes gentler elements in Marlowe and witty juxtaposing of fancy and observation.

LEWIS, C. S. "*Hero and Leander,*" *Proceedings of the British Academy,* XXXVIII (1952), 23–37. Chapman's poem and Marlowe's poem complement each other, "like passing from a Song of Innocence to a Song of Experience."

SMITH, HALLETT. "Ovidian Poetry." *Elizabethan Poetry, A Study in Conventions, Meaning, and Expression.* Cambridge, Mass.: Harvard University Press, 1952. Emphasizes the "highly romantic or baroque decoration" in the poem.

Index

Index

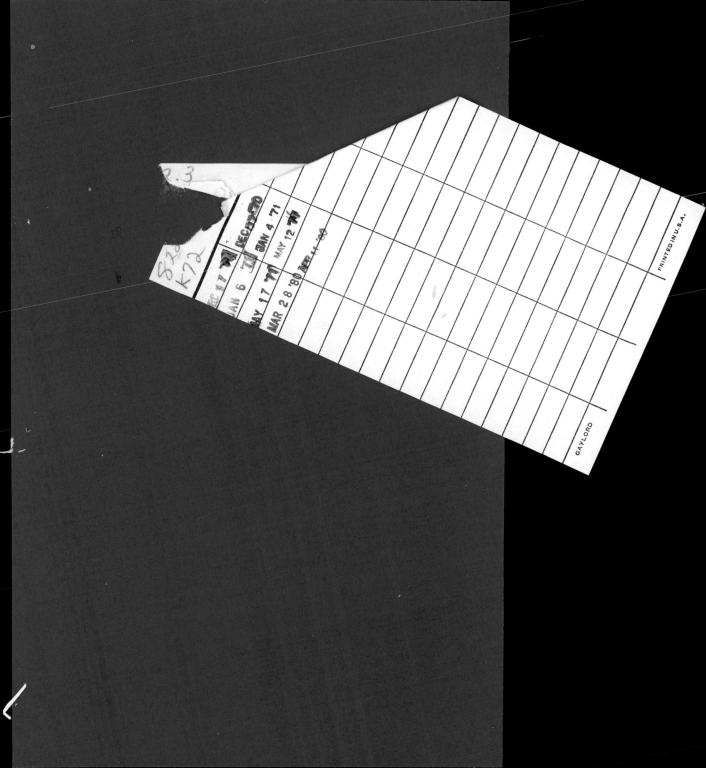